# REAL GHOST STORIES

HAUNTING

ENCOUNTERS

TOLD BY

REAL PEOPLE

TONY & JENNY BRUESKI

Ulysses Press

Collection and editorial copyright © 2017 Real Story Media Inc.
Design and concept copyright © 2017 Ulysses Press and its licensors.
Ghost stories are reprinted with the story author's permission. All
rights reserved. Any unauthorized duplication in whole or in part or
dissemination of this edition by any means (including but not limited to
photocopying, electronic devices, digital versions, and the Internet) will
be prosecuted to the fullest extent of the law.

Published in the United States by:
Ulysses Press
P.O. Box 3440
Berkeley, CA 94703
www.ulyssespress.com

ISBN: 978-1-61243-715-6
Library of Congress Catalog Number 2017938178

Printed in Canada by Marquis Book Publishing
10 9 8 7 6 5 4 3 2 1

Acquisitions editor: Casie Vogel
Managing editor: Claire Chun
Editor: Shayna Keyles
Proofreader: Lauren Harrison
Layout: Caety Klingman
Front cover design: Malea Clark-Nicholson
Artwork from shutterstock.com: abandoned house © Slava Gerj; moon
    (cover) © O.Bellini; moon (interior) © Daniel Fung; clouds © warat42

Distributed by Publishers Group West

*Dedicated to the millions of "paranormally affected" individuals around the world who have chosen our show as the venue to tell your stories. We are humbled by your listenership and patronage.*

# CONTENTS

# INTRODUCTION: WHY WE'RE HERE

So, here we are. Together at last. You and your desire to read creepy ghost stories, and our need to share them. If you want to jump straight to the ghost stories, then by all means, skip ahead to the next chapters. We won't judge.

However, if you're one of those people who wants to understand where the stories are coming from and how this network of thousands of "paranormally affected" people came to be, then stick around. This is the chapter to put it all into context.

Let's begin with a little background on the podcast that inspired this book—our podcast, *Real Ghost Stories Online*.

For those of you not familiar with what a podcast is, don't worry, it's not complicated. It's a radio show that you can download on your mobile device or computer through a provider like iTunes or Spotify. It's set up very similarly to a talk radio show, except we don't drone on and on with political banter or extreme opinions. We spend an hour on each episode talking about ghosts, and that's it. Just ghosts.

We take calls from people who share their stories, we read letters sent to us about real encounters with the paranormal, and then we discuss the stories.

The show has become a platform for people to share their real encounters with the paranormal, without judgment or reprisal. It is also a way to feel normal, where listeners can take in other experiences that may not be so different from their own.

## WHO ARE WE?

The hosts (that's us, Tony and Jenny Brueski) aren't scientists, medical professionals, or paranormal investigators. We're a husband and wife team that have always had an interest in the topic of the paranormal and we love to hear others' stories of their encounters with things that go bump in the night. We don't take ourselves too seriously, either. If you are a regular listener, you already know this by the thousands of references to '80s television series, interludes of soft-rock hits from the '70s, or the many other paths the conversations seem to take on a daily basis. Bottom line, we are regular people who talk about a not-so-regular topic. The following chapters will give you a chance to get to know us better on an individual level, including the experiences we've personally had with the paranormal, which fuel our curiosity.

The concept for *Real Ghost Stories Online* was a bit of an accident. Every Halloween when Tony was working in FM radio, he would ask the audience to call in their ghost stories. The "Ghost Show" was always his favorite to host and would generate the most calls of almost any topic all year. The problem was, he could only get away with doing a show on this subject matter once a year. He wanted more and knew the audience did, too. Eventually, YouTube came around, and Tony started to post the audio from each year's episode there. We were shocked by the volume of views these would receive year round.

This proved to us that there was an audience for a radio show like ours outside of Halloween. So Tony decided to try something new, to do the show he'd always wanted to do, and moved his on-air life from FM radio to a podcast. No more "weather and traffic next." We started podcasting full-time on a topic that we love. What a journey it has become, and one that we don't want to end anytime soon.

Over the last few years, we have heard thousands of ghost stories and talked with thousands of people who have lived through some very unexplained circumstances. Some are much more disturbing than others.

## WHAT KEEPS US UP AT NIGHT

We are often asked what our "most disturbing" story on the show has been, and it's always hard to come up with an answer. However, there is one story that haunts us more than most; it was a series of calls from a man in the South. His story still troubles us to this day.

In his initial call to our show, he told us how he and his wife had been searching for their first home together, and in that search, they found something that was hardly more than a foreclosed fixer-upper. The home they settled on had bare floorboards, walls that needed extensive repair, and it generally required quite a bit of time and attention. When the caller first walked into the house, he described the air as being thick, almost as if he were wading through water, yet he brushed it off as nerves.

Shortly after moving in, he woke up to find every cabinet door and drawer in his kitchen wide open and one of his children's toys activated in the center of the floor, where it had not been the night prior. When talking with his wife, she claimed not to have had anything to do with the odd scene. He dismissed this for a moment. Soon after, however, a visiting friend fled the home, leaving the door ajar as he ran to the street. Apparently, he had heard the voices of two people arguing in an adjacent room, which had been empty at the time.

Many more unexplained occurrences followed. Late one night, the entity let itself be known. Our caller claimed that he felt pinned down in his bed in a bout of sleep paralysis; unsure of whether the experience was paranormal or not, he awoke in a panic and calmed himself. His calm was short-lived, however, as that same night, his wife woke him, terrified by what she had witnessed in the hall leading to the bedrooms. She claimed to have seen a short man, as dark as a solid shadow, wearing a cloak embedded with unusual patterns and symbols that she did not understand. Frightened and confused, the family fled the house in the middle of the night.

This was the end of his first call and the end of his story, for all we knew. Being new to regularly hosting a show like this, we didn't know what to expect or think. We felt horrible for this man and his family, but honestly, we didn't expect to hear a follow-up, and for his sake, we hoped we wouldn't. We wanted the horror this family experienced to end, and assumed that maybe it had.

Then, a few weeks later, a second call came in from the same man. He was thankful for our feedback and for giving him a judgment-free outlet for sharing what many would look at as a crazy experience. He explained that while he would have liked to move out of the home, they were not in a financial situation to do so. That's why after he and his wife fled the house, he'd contacted someone to have the house blessed and cleansed. Though hopes were running high, he didn't feel that the cleansing had worked. The paranormal activity seemed to grow stronger and more intense, targeting his children and wife on a more frequent basis.

Desperate for a solution, he'd hired a paranormal investigation group to visit the home. The team spent some time researching the property and its history. They found that the former owners of the home simply left and never returned, putting the house back in the hands of the bank that eventually sold it to our caller at a discounted rate. The researchers attempted to locate the former owners to ask them questions, but could not locate them after weeks of digging. This was quite mysterious in itself, and it left us wondering what they knew about the property and what experiences they had while living there.

In the following weeks and months, the family members experienced dramatic mood changes while living in the house; they were so extreme that the caller described his wife as "not being the same person" that she was when they moved in. He was about to expand on this when suddenly his phone simply cut out, and the story was over.

This was not the first time this occurred. Maybe three out of his four calls into our show would end in an abrupt cutout, making the call unusable on air. What made these hang ups unusual was the fact that it was not the caller choosing to hang up, as happens when one is nervous or gets off topic. These were hard drops, as if the line were simply cut off. One could conclude that something didn't want this story to get out.

The most haunting call we received from this man was his third submission. His tone was clearly distraught as he shared the latest update on his home and life. He'd attempted to have a medium come into the house to try and discover what was going on, and possibly lead to a solution to the paranormal problems. The medium only went as far as opening a closet door, before she gasped and quickly exited the home, apologizing and stating that she couldn't help. Frustrated, the family attempted to continue living their lives with this unknown presence in their home. The family dog began to growl at unseen entities, and the family members continued to experience extreme mood shifts.

While he was describing the activity in the house, an unexplained and eerie breeze-like sound overtook the background of the call for a few seconds. It was unlike anything we had heard on any pervious call. Our initial thought was that maybe he opened a patio door while talking on the phone. However, he later confirmed that he had not moved and no sounds were present in the background while he was calling us. It was him, and him alone, on a couch in a silent room.

What happened after we initially aired this call is one of the most shocking things we've ever experienced with our audience. Almost immediately, we began to receive calls and letters from listeners reporting that they started to feel sick to their stomachs as soon as the unexplained noise came on the air. It's important to note that we received these reports before we made a point of discussing the sound or bringing attention to it in a follow-up episode. That means that these calls and letters were unsolicited observations from multiple people, in different parts of the world, who all experienced the same physical reaction to the story at the same time. How this occurred, we don't know. We're just glad that we weren't personally or physically affected the way so many others were. To this day, we get letters from new listeners of the show who hear this episode and experience the same symptoms.

The fourth call we received from this man brought a personal revelation to the story. While moving some items at his mother's house, he discovered a massive chest with strange imagery and engravings lining the outside. He wanted to look inside, but it was locked. After a little tinkering with the lock, he was able to open the lid to reveal the contents inside. What he found shocked and disturbed him.

The dark, massive chest was filled with items one would only associate with the occult: locks of hair, black magic books, summoning books, demonic books, books on how to "redeem" someone's faith, and pictures of groups of women wearing black robes. In several of these pictures stood his mother.

When looking through the books, he found a symbol that resonated with him. It was the very same symbol that his mother had allowed him to get as a tattoo in his youth. The only symbol his mother had allowed him to get tattooed in his youth. He didn't know what the symbol meant, but he'd been excited to get the tattoo. The symbol was then forever etched on his body with the consent and knowledge of his mother.

In the mysterious chest, he also discovered pictures of himself as a child with a forgotten childhood playmate. He got in touch with the old friend, and they met for lunch to discuss their memories of growing up. They discovered that they shared the same symbol tattooed on their bodies. What all this meant was still in question. With all the activity in his home, he felt these discoveries were likely all tied together.

Paranormal activity continued to plague him and his family. One night, his daughter's covers were torn off of her bed and thrown to the opposite wall. A dark entity screamed in her face while she struggled to sleep. Our caller was very frustrated and confused and had no idea what to do. Every attempt to defeat or stop these events failed.

That was the last we heard from him. Months later, we received an unsolicited and mysterious call from a voice just stating that they knew who the caller was, and that his stories were true. Whatever happened to him and his family remains a mystery to us to this day. We can only hope and pray that things calmed down and they are all right.

One other story that came into our show still mystifies us. The call came to us from a woman who sounded very troubled by a haunting experience. The problem with the call was that it seemed like she was trying to share her story while putting dishes away—every dish she ever owned, it seemed, with loud clinking and distracting bangs throughout her entire story. This made it extremely hard to focus on her story or give constructive feedback.

After we aired her story, she reached back out to us and told us that what occurred on her call was one of the biggest problems she had been experiencing: the inability to share what was going on in her life. When she would call friends or write letters, something would interfere with the transmission, just like what occurred on her call to us. When we listened back to the call, we picked up on more than just the sounds of dishes clanking. There was clear evidence to electronic voice phenomena (EVP), growls, and other bizarre audio anomalies in her story.

The content of the story involved seeing a dark, cloaked figure standing near her room at night and the feeling of oppression as these events would occur. We continued to get updates from her and her friends for several months. At one point, the oppression on this poor woman led to what some could speculate was borderline possession. The good news was that the oppressive entity seemed to have moved away, and she did get back to her normal self. We can only hope that it stayed that way.

## WHO'S CALLING, PLEASE?

Why did we receive these strange calls in the first few months of creating our show? What happened to those involved in these stories? Will we ever have another story with such audible evidence of a haunting in it again? These are questions that we ask ourselves quite often when recording our podcast.

It has truly been an incredible journey hosting this show, and we are just getting started. We can only speculate on what we may be talking about five, ten, or even twenty years. We also wonder if we will be any closer to identifying the phenomena that cause these hauntings, which plague millions of people all over the world. Will we ever be able to truly identify the cause and take control of these situations from a scientific standpoint, or will we still look back on these stories and wonder for hundreds of years to come? Either way, we hope our show can be considered one of the largest, most detailed repositories of haunted experiences for those seeking the answers to this question.

With that, we welcome you to this book and our show. In comparison to the number of stories we have heard and archived, this book contains about 1/1,000,000 of them. If you like what you hear, there is so much more to take in on our podcast and websites. For now, though, sit back, relax, and enjoy this journey into *Real Ghost Stories*.

# CHAPTER 1
# DON'T LISTEN TO STRANGERS

Growing up, one of the most common phrases you heard was very likely "don't talk to strangers." We always felt the concept of "don't listen to strangers" was just as important.

Over the years, many of our listeners have come know our backgrounds and quirks. If you're new to our brand of paranormal discussion, welcome! We thought it would be good to stop being strangers. We'll start off by giving you a little backstory on who we are and where we come from to help you better understand our voices and opinions on the unexplained topics we are about to get into. If you already know us from the podcast, here is a chance to learn a little more about the strange voices that travel with you every day as you listen.

# SEEKING THE DEAD: TONY BRUESKI'S STORY

In some of my first childhood memories, I am often doing one of two things, and at times combining the two: playing "radio station" or "being a ghostbuster." I was an only child, so that left plenty of time for my mind to wander and allowed me to develop into a very creative and curious individual. I still have a cassette tape that my aunt recorded on one of those old black rectangular tape decks of me at the age of two playing "Ghostbuster Radio."

I guess that could be considered the earliest incarnation of the show.

To say that I am doing what I love, or what I was meant to do, may be a bit of an understatement. The interest in the topic of ghosts and my passion for broadcasting seemed to have started from the moment I could speak. As for why these are deeply ingrained interests, I'm not sure, as many of the life events that kept me interested in the topic occurred many years after I made my initial broadcasts to the family pets.

In this chapter, I'm going to take you back to some of the paranormal encounters that made me the person you hear today, and maybe answer some of your questions about the random thoughts that come out of my mouth on our podcast. I must forewarn you, however: Unlike on the podcast, there will not be any quiche recipes in this chapter. If you came here searching for the most kick-ass egg-in-a-pie-crust recipe ever, this would be a letdown. Now that we have that out of the way, let's begin.

I grew up in the medium-sized town of Fond du Lac, Wisconsin, located about evenly between Milwaukee and Green Bay. It was a great environment for exploring. We sat on one of the largest inland lakes in the country, had miles of hiking and walking trails, and even had a storied history of mob legends and historical figures wandering through our city.

I loved walking around the downtown area, which was dotted sporadically with some antiquated stores. When I was a child, my mom would push me in the stroller past the now-vacant shops she once frequented and tell me stories of their former retail lives. I would peer into those windows wondering what once was, enthralled by the peeling paint and decaying walls visible through the glass. I was fortunate enough to witness firsthand a few holdouts before time would claim them, as well.

There also stands a historic hotel building in this downtown that I would wander through as a teenager. It's allegedly home to a resident ghost named Walter, who was the creator of the building around the turn of the century. Walter apparently saw fit to reverse his name and give it to the property, adding to the building's spooky factor: Retlaw.

There was certainly a creepy undertone to many of the places my mother would take me to visit and explore, and I loved every minute of it. They are some of my fondest memories, and I wouldn't change them for anything. One of my other favorite places to visit with my mother was called Rienzi Cemetery, a sprawling graveyard lined with oak, hickory, and black walnut trees. To get there, we would never take the main road; instead, we would follow a shortcut. It was a journey that started at the edge of the woods in my backyard and involved scaling a large rock ledge in the middle of a forest, then wandering through several valleys lined with dead grapevines, trees that had been uprooted by storms, fallen branches, dead leaves, and a desolate creek. Eventually, we would reach the back of the cemetery and find ourselves in one of the eeriest settings a person could put themselves in.

I'd find myself peering into a hundred-plus-year-old cemetery filled with massive trees, dilapidated gravestones, and not a single living human in sight. From there, I would wander into the graveyard to explore, read the dates on the headstones, and soak in the creepy atmosphere for every second that I was there. As an excuse to stay in the cemetery longer, we would collect fallen hickory nuts from the trees to take home for later cracking. We would often wrap up our walks around dusk, just in time for me to return to my basement "studio," which consisted of a WTCX bumper sticker and a bulky boom box. Here I would talk about my experiences while playing "Today's Hits and Yesterday's Favorites" for my number-one listener, my cat Murphy.

Eventually, I grew out of playing radio station, and at the age of fourteen, I found myself employed by the very same radio station I had pretended to be on for the previous eleven years of my life. I got the job after being a guest DJ for an hour during a station promotion. The station general manager, Terry Davis, called, asking, "Who is this kid?!" and hired me on the spot. I would spend the next five years practically living at the station, doing every job I possibly could while soaking up the creepiness of downtown. There were many moments during this time span where I could have easily been canned from my radio job for pulling some adolescent on-air stunt, but thanks to the patience and understanding of my bosses Todd Dehring and Gregg Owens, I was allowed to continue and make my passion into my lifelong career.

The radio studio had a large storefront window that overlooked Main Street. That's where we would do our shows, and where we were able to view the vibrant nightlife of one of the drunkest cities in the United States. It was also the location where I first hosted a real, on-air ghost show. Every Halloween, I would take calls and discuss local legends and haunts. This would eventually lead me to do a little ghost exploring of my own. The best place to start just happened to be in the basement of the radio station itself.

Housed in what had been a carriage stop, tavern, and countless other businesses over the last hundred years, the radio station had quite a history and a few ghosts of its own. From the basement, one could enter what had once been a tunnel that led to other locations in the area. Now bricked off, you were very limited as to the depths you could explore. I had always been told it was part of the Underground Railroad, but some historians now argue that it may have been part of a bootlegging tunnel during prohibition. Either way, it held energy, as did the rest of the building.

I was "lucky" enough to only have had one paranormal experience at my first radio station, while many that I worked with had multiple, such as hearing the sounds of children playing in the halls, observing keyboards typing on their own, and seeing mysterious figures walking past windowed doors to dead ends, never to be seen again.

My experience occurred on a Sunday afternoon, when I was alone in the building.

I was sitting at my desk working on the computer when I heard the familiar sound of keys and shifting papers going down the hall. This was a sound I was accustomed to hearing on a regular basis when our news director, Greg Stensland, headed past my door to his studio. Thinking nothing of these sounds, I simply went on working for a minute, then decided I would take a break and chat for a moment with Greg down the hall. As I got up and made my way down the hall, something odd struck me. No lights were on in the studio area. "Greg would never work in the dark," I thought. But I continued forward. As I turned the corner to say hello, I was met with an empty, dark studio, with only the glow of an Associated Press computer dimly lighting the corner of the room. No Greg, no noises, nothing.

What had I just heard? Who walked past my door? I didn't know what to think. More than a little creeped out, I left my office for the day and didn't return until other living souls were also in the building the following Monday.

My next encounter with the unexplained would occur a few years later when I was living alone in my first apartment in Wausau, Wisconsin. I define this as "unexplained" rather than paranormal, because to this day, I'm not sure what it was.

My apartment was located above a bookstore on the square in the downtown area. All around this square stood historic buildings, many of which had documented hauntings within them. These buildings included a historic theater, an apartment building that was formerly a sister hotel to the aforementioned Retlaw of my hometown, and several other businesses. Behind my bedroom wall was a staircase that led to the upstairs of a sporting goods store. On this staircase, some have claimed to have seen the image of a woman carrying a child from level to level. When I had my experience, I was unaware of any of these stories.

A few months into living at my apartment, something startled me awake. I do not know what broke my sleep, but it did cause me to sit up in bed. At this moment, I suddenly felt paralyzed. A freezing sensation took over me as what felt like a cloud slowly lurked through the front of my body and out the back. I could not move or open my eyes as this terrifying moment played out. The experience lasted only seconds, but it felt like hours. After I had regained control of myself, I slumped back into my bed, hid under the covers, and eventually fell back asleep.

The following day, I contacted a paranormal investigator to ask about the history of my building and the area. It was in this conversation over pizza that I learned about sleep paralysis and the haunted history of my city block, with its haunted theater and other businesses.

Was it sleep paralysis?

I don't know. There are elements of it that seem to fit that diagnosis and others that do not. The fact that I was able to sit up before feeling paralyzed makes me question it being sleep paralysis alone. The history of the area makes me question this assessment as well. Either way, it was the closest and most personal experience I've ever had that may be defined as paranormal.

The years following this experience would be spent living the nomadic life of a radio DJ, hosting radio shows on various stations throughout Wisconsin, Michigan, Washington, and Kansas. My interest in the paranormal would take a spot on the back burner outside of my yearly Halloween show. The audio from these once-a-year Halloween episodes would be the building blocks to the show you hear today.

With the advent of YouTube, I began taking audio from my Halloween radio show and posting it for the world to hear. My expectations were nonexistent. After a few years of posting these shows, I noticed that their view count was well into the hundreds of thousands, with hundreds of comments asking for more shows. This shocked me and led to what I call the light bulb moment for creating *Real Ghost Stories Online*.

Podcasting had begun to establish itself as a serious platform for broadcasting topics of specific interests. I thought to myself, why not start a weekly podcast about ghost stories in the same vein as my Halloween shows? Nothing was holding me back from doing this, other than myself! I just needed to do it. The first episodes of *Real Ghost Stories Online* were built on previous content used on my FM radio shows. Interviews and callers were all recycled from years past, and I asked the audience for new ghost stories. Luckily, I found a cohost in Jenny, and we found an audience. Calls and letters began flowing in, and we had a show! A show that has changed my life, and the way I view our existence.

Today, the show has grown from once a week to four days a week and has been downloaded millions of times worldwide. While many things in my life have been a surprise, I can honestly say that I never expected this show to grow to the level it has in such a short period. I am incredibly grateful to our loyal audience and look forward to many more years of sharing and discussing *Real Ghost Stories*!

## WHO IS THAT QUIET LITTLE GIRL?: JENNY BRUESKI'S STORY

I remember people would slow down as they drove by the elementary school, sometimes pointing at her—the little girl that sat alone playing jacks on the steps of the old stone school house, her long, light brown hair pulled back into braids. Her dress, very different from those of the other school kids on the playground, was a style that could have been from fifty years ago. She liked the dresses that would fly out as she twirled. Sometimes, the teachers who kept guard as the children played would peek around the side of the schoolhouse to see what the passersby were slowing to see. They could see her too. One tall, lovely teacher even sat near the little girl. "I bet they think they see a ghost," she would casually say in her east Texas drawl. The little girl didn't quite understand what the teacher meant by this comment, and just shrugged, never missing her hand at jacks.

Any mention of ghosts to an elementary schoolgirl should have sparked a sudden chill or ping of fear, but not for this little girl. They were just a part of life, as much as the fire ant hills that she would accidentally step into on occasion; she may not have liked them, but they would always turn up. She paused her game to take a peek at the brush burn on the side of her hand from the repeated scooping of the jacks. Still processing what the teacher had said, she timidly spoke. "Do you believe in ghosts, Mrs. Barnes?"

"Naw, darlin', there's no such thing," the teacher said with a giggle. "But, I do believe some people are old souls. I think you might be an old soul," she added, standing to check on the other children.

Not knowing what an old soul was, the little girl asked, "Does that mean I might know people from a long time ago?" The teacher looked back at the girl, a little perplexed by the response, then simply said, "Come on now, we're fixin' to go back in." The girl quickly gathered up her silver jacks and faded pink rubber ball and put them back into their light green striped bag, where they were safe until tomorrow's recess.

One might have thought there was something not quite right with her, or something that troubled her, by the way she loved to play in the shadows of the schoolyard pecan tree. When she tried to teach them how to crack the nuts for a recess treat, the other children just looked at her with a cruel, confused look, before running away to mindlessly garner more blisters on the monkey bars. But she was a good girl, and she was quiet, so she didn't require the attention of her teachers. They just let her be. I guess to truly understand why the little girl seemed happier on the schoolhouse steps alone, playing a game that was outdated a half-century ago, you would have to know the story of when she was the least lonely. You would have to understand the friendship that she found years ago, or rather, how it found her.

It was a muggy day without a breath of wind. The kind of day that made you glad for the shade of the loblolly pines, despite their endless weeping of sap. The little girl sat quietly on her tire swing in her typical backyard uniform of denim overalls, with her long hair pulled into high pigtails and her trusty homemade slingshot in her front chest pocket. She was swaying ever so slightly on the swing, listening intently for the slightest whisper of a distant train. In those days, the highlight of her day was the freight train that would pass directly behind the cedar fence at the far edge of her backyard. It was a game for her to see how long she could stay outside as the train passed before becoming so frightened by the thundering roar of the engines that she'd run inside. Even at that age, she loved to tempt her fears. But so far that day, there was no train. Only the deafening sound of locusts high in the trees filled the air. Her tire swing slowly turned to face the far corner of her backyard, and she was startled to see someone was there.

A small, innocent, pale face peered around the corner of her brick home. He had brown eyes shaded by a funny hat, the likes of which she had never seen before. She could tell from his height he was probably a couple of years older than her, and he was as solid and real as anyone. "Hey," she called out as she slid down from her dirty side-of-the-road tire swing. He didn't say a word back, but he didn't run either. He slowly stepped out from behind the bricks, and just stood there, as startled to see her as she was to see him. He had funny clothes. At least, they were funny to a five year old who had never seen a child wear suspenders. He pushed back his newsboy hat as he wiped the sweat from his forehead. Then, completely fearless, she said the words that would change the course of her future.

"You wanna play?" she asked. His eyes grew large, and in an "I thought you'd never ask" tone, he simply said, "Yep."

Whenever she told anyone about the boy in the yard, she was always met with "Oh, that's sweet, you have an imaginary friend." Imaginary friend was not a term that she was familiar with, so she went along with whatever the grown-ups said for their sake, not hers. And she talked about him a lot, telling everyone of the fun they had on their latest backyard adventure. No one seemed too curious or concerned about her new-found friendship. They never asked her too many questions, so minimal details about the boy were shared; but they did ask one thing. "What is his name?" The little girl, honestly, had never asked him. She blurted out the name "Jack," like she knew it all along. And through the dirty glass on the patio door, she saw him nodding his head in approval. Either he liked the name, or it was shared with her in a way that she couldn't possibly understand.

For the better part of a year, they were inseparable. They played on the tire swing or had tea parties, where the only thing imaginary was the tea. He was always willing to selflessly play anything that she wanted. But that could be chalked up to the fact that she'd rather take aim at a squirrel with her slingshot than play baby dolls. She did, however, force him to pretend to be the happy groom at the end of the aisle as she paraded toward him in her flowing gown made of Charmin toilet paper. He gladly played this out more times than the little girl could count. The truth is that she truly couldn't imagine going back to playing without him, and in her naivety, she thought if they "married," he would always be there, ready to play in the backyard. And he was always there, seemingly as glad for her company as she was for his.

Then one stifling hot summer day, it all changed. As the two were lazily sitting on the swings of her rusty A-frame swing set, he suddenly said, "I gotta be goin' soon." She looked at him, and giggling, said, "You never go anywhere."

"Naw, its time. I gotta go to Oklahoma." he said, as he was kicking the dirt with his lace-up boot. She looked at him, puzzled as to why he had to leave, but even more confused by where he said he was going. "What is a Oklahoma?" she asked, having never heard the word before.

"It's another place, kinda like Texas."

As tears began to well up in her green eyes, she simply said, "Why?"

"It's time, and you got to start goin' to school soon," he replied. He looked as sad at the prospect of leaving as she was at the idea of being left.

"When are you goin'?" she whispered through the lump in her throat.

"I have to go now." Then, he got up and walked over to the edge of the backyard. He turned and gave her an impish smile once more, then faded as he walked through the cedar fence.

You might think that is where this story ends, but truth be told, it's where her story really started. To say that she was a loner would be an understatement. She tried to bond with the other children in her class or in her after-school activities, but she never seemed to completely allow herself to experience true friendship again. As the years went by, she found comfort in her trusty jacks and the old stone schoolhouse porch, and anything that reminded her of him. She didn't need the other kids, and they didn't need her. There was a wisdom about her that made the games the other children played seem trivial. She could never break through the maturity beyond her years.

As the little girl grew into a young woman, she eventually retired her overalls and pigtails. The loneliness hung on, though. She would try to be social, and participate in activities with her classmates, but mostly she found herself bound to her schoolwork. She was a very good student, and enjoyed studying history the most. And gradually over time, she began to think about Jack less and less. Growing up was a full-time job, and she felt a little ashamed that she still missed her imaginary friend from all those years ago. Eventually, she forgot about Jack.

After years of never completely being understood, she finally found someone that got her. He understood her affinity toward all things old, and the quirkiness of her personality, and even the loneliness that had become ingrained in her. His ability to be either playful or mature, depending on circumstances, fit well with her dual nature. They were both wise beyond their years, but equally enjoyed each other's humor. In ways he reminded her of Jack, in that he didn't expect her to be anyone other than who she was. And she finally began to feel the true, vulnerable friendship that she had lost so long ago. This time when she married it was for real, and the dress was not made of Charmin.

He was bold. He was always willing to try the unexpected or try to beat the odds against whatever venture he had set in his mind, whereas she would always shy away from trying anything that might not work out as expected. He nevertheless always encouraged her to be bold as well. But bold was not how she was wired. It took a lot of prodding for him to convince her to come out of her shell and join him for an hour in his claustrophobic office to work on his latest project: listening to and discussing ghost stories, of all things. She had never spent any real time in front of a microphone, but what scared her most was that she believed in ghosts and had always considered them just a part of life. So the thought of listening to real ghost stories terrified her more than any Hollywood horror plot. It never crossed her mind that this was what she was born to do.

After the first couple of episodes, the topic of imaginary friends came up. He shared that he'd had an imaginary friend, but always knew it was conjured up in his imagination, and was never actually visible. She thought back to all those years ago and began to tell about Jack—someone who was very real to her, and as visible as she was. She told of how she met Jack and of how Jack left her. After she finished telling of her first friend, her husband Tony sat there in silence, before he said, "People don't really see their imaginary friends. Not to mention ones that dress from a different time period." It was in that moment that Jenny realized she had a ghost story to share, too.

# CHAPTER 2
# HAUNTED HOUSES

Chances are that when you think "ghost stories," an image of a rickety old abandoned house comes to mind. While these can be the setting for a number of troubling haunting accounts, they are not always the key ingredient. In fact, it seems that homes of any age can come down with a haunting. In some cases, there doesn't appear to be any definable trait that makes a home likely to be haunted, other than the fact that the home exists. This leads us down the road of exploring the land a home sits on, the people that pass through it, the objects in it, and the history of what once stood in its place.

Once we can examine all of these elements, there is usually a clue or two that may lead us to diagnose where the haunting originates from. It's not the question of whether the house is haunted that is most difficult to answer; rather, the question of how to get rid of the haunting poses the most problems.

## LIVING WITH THE DEAD

In our opinion, one of the most common misconceptions about ghosts is that they are very "one-dimensional" in their thinking and actions. Often, people tend to categorize a spirit as simply good or bad; we, too, are guilty of this at times. However, just as living and breathing souls aren't always good or bad one hundred percent of the time, we believe that ghosts aren't, either.

This reality can lead to confusion, as the actions of a ghost may be viewed as helpful one day and troubling or aggressive the next. People will often assume there is more than one spirit involved when different phenomena are taking place, but it could all be from the same ghost.

As you will discover in our next story, a protective ghost may be to blame for the unexplained activity. These spirits may be acting not just to protect the property they once inhabited, but to protect well-being of those who live there today.

The following is a letter sent to us from Charlie L. about his relationship-saving experience with the undead.

> I am a professional land surveyor in Michigan. I received my education from a university located in a small town in the same state.
>
> In the fall of 2000, I moved into my first off-campus residence with a group of new friends from my previous year in the dorm. We had rented an old farmhouse that sits adjacent to the university. All evidence of the farm was long since lost, having been engulfed by mixed residential and commercial properties. Even so, the farmhouse was clearly older than all the surrounding structures were. It had features that showed its age, most notably the large cistern in the basement that used

to collect rainwater for the household and the single bathroom on the main level. The bathroom appeared to be an afterthought to the home, as the home was probably originally serviced with an outhouse. The farmhouse also had what is locally known as a Michigan Basement, a basement made of large rocks mortared together. They have low ceilings and are always damp and dark.

The home was long from front to back. There were plank hardwood floors throughout, but they had been covered with commercial-grade carpeting everywhere except for the long hallway connecting the living room and kitchen. The house had old windows with glass full of wavy imperfections from a bygone manufacturing process. There were three bedrooms upstairs and a single bedroom on the main level, adjacent to the living room.

Let's be clear about one thing. This home was a dump. The landlord had neglected it for years and rented it out to college students at ridiculously high rates. My roommates did not exactly help matters. It did not take long for them to start doing damage to the home. They opened holes in the walls, played hockey with full cans of tuna, and removed now-obsolete cast-iron steam registers for their scrap metal, causing a good amount of damage to floors and the roof. Yes, the roof. That is a whole other story.

Anyway, we had been in the home for about a month when odd things started happening. The first thing we noticed were the doors slamming shut during the night. These were old farmhouse doors, and they were hung to protect the old hardwood floors. Since carpet was on the floor, it took a grown man yanking with two hands to close these doors. They were intended to stay open, as they only separated interior common spaces. We'd all be in bed and you would hear them slam close. We would all confer in the morning to check that no one had been playing tricks on each other. Plus, we had all tried to slam these doors, and no one could replicate it.

Then, the nighttime noises started. Lots of knocking sounds and noises that sounded like people walking on the creaky old wood floors. We all laughed about it and started to like the idea that there may be a ghost in the house. Soon the ghost became a favorite excuse for house issues. We would joke that "the ghost" ate the last box of macaroni and cheese dinner, or it was supposed to be the ghost's turn to do the dishes. Simple things to ease the underlying anxiety of having a spirit reside with you.

Then, my out-of-town girlfriend started visiting. This was when the ghost took a different attitude. Her first night in the house, she got up to use the bathroom, which was downstairs from my bedroom. When she walked into the hall, she saw a woman round the corner and head down the stairs. She ran back into my room and woke me up. My response was to go downstairs and investigate. I found nothing out of place or any people that shouldn't be there. However, she was convinced that she had seen a woman. She was so terrified that she refused to go downstairs by herself to use the bathroom for the next two years. I always had to escort her.

Things continued as they were for the two years we lived in the house. We always laughed it away and thought the idea of a ghost was fun.

One day toward the end of our lease, I was alone in the house with a female friend of mine, who was not my girlfriend. It was late afternoon, and massive thunderstorms were moving through the area. We sat in the living room watching TV on the couch. Just when things could've taken a turn toward romantic, there were three slow, solid bangs on the bedroom door behind me.

I leaped off the couch and toward the locked bedroom door, which was a mere two steps behind me. Again, there were two solid thuds on the door. I was able to put my hand on the door and feel the vibration for the second thud.

My lady friend was scared and standing on the opposite side of the living room. Being logical, I wanted an explanation for this. Having a ghost as a joke is one thing, but this was real. I was witnessing it. I could not brush it off as just a mysterious noise in the dead of night. I ran outside into the thunderstorm to inspect the bedroom windows. I figured that the storm must've broken one of the windows and the wind was causing the door to thud from the inside out.

Once I made it out the door to investigate, I stood there in the rain dumbfounded. Everything was intact. I walked back indoors without an explanation. I drove my friend back to her dorm and returned to my house. When my roommate returned that Sunday night, I made sure I was present when he unlocked his door. Sure enough, everything was normal. There was absolutely nothing out of place and I could find no logical reason for the noise.

All these years later, I have to wonder if the ghost was doing me a favor. I was still dating my long-distance girlfriend at the time and had always been loyal to her. If I had caved to my friend's advance, I would've ruined our loyalty. I have now been with that girlfriend for seventeen years and have been married to her for eleven. I am so glad that I did not tarnish our relationship that day, so I guess I owe that ghost a solid.

# DEMON HANDS

An unexpected in-home encounter with wildlife can sometimes arouse suspicion of ghosts. Ghosts can also be dismissed in the same way: It's much easier to accept that there's a pack of raccoons clawing away in the attic than the spirit of the former tenant or a lost child still begging to be let out. In more cases than not, the paranormal activity is explained away without investigation and is blamed on animals.

Some, however, take the step of investigating the sounds that they hear. They take the time to narrow down the possibilities, not with the intent of debunking the supernatural. Rather, they just want to get firm answers. This is always the best plan of attack when an unknown noise is plaguing the residents of the home. It's better to know the cause of the sounds than to blindly speculate on what may be going on. Even if the conclusion ends with the suspicion of ghosts.

The next story is one of a classic haunted house. Individuals are plagued by unexplained sounds and suspect wildlife, only to discover something very different. Jesse shares the story:

This specific story affected my life, my relationships, and my work. I had met a young woman whom I started dating. She lived thirty minutes outside of Fort Wayne, Indiana, where I resided. I wanted to move closer to her, so I uprooted myself and moved to Huntington, Indiana. When I first moved there, I was jobless and homeless, so my girlfriend's mother offered me a place to stay, at least until I found a job and my own place. I stayed there a few months and finally found a job, saved up some money, and started looking for a place. I found a two-bedroom duplex and took the second floor. When I moved in, it wasn't in that great a shape, but it was a cheap rental. This was the beginning of a six-month-long living hell!

My friends dubbed the duplex "The House on Hill Road." I had been living there for two weeks when I had finally settled in and decided to throw a housewarming party. I invited a bunch of friends, including my brother Steven and my friend Chase. The party had kicked off with lots of drinking, beer pong, kings cup, and joking, and everyone appeared to be having a good time. I had worked a ten-hour shift that day and decided to turn in early. About an hour later, my girlfriend crawled into bed with me.

Ten minutes later, I got a knock on my bedroom door. Slightly buzzed and in the middle of intimacy, I was, of course, a little pissed off. So I yelled, "What! I'm busy." It was my brother. Apparently, he and my friend Chase decided to rummage through my attic. He had been cut on top of his foot.

I opened the door and sure enough, he's bleeding on my damn carpet. "How in the fuck!" I said. He responded, "Bro, I don't know. I didn't even feel it, 'til we came down." I told him to clean that scrap up. "You better not stain my carpet, or we are fighting."

This is where it gets interesting.

The next morning, I got up to discover that many of the partygoers from the night before were passed out everywhere. My brother was up playing Xbox, so I asked him to come up to the attic with me so we could have a look around.

This attic is old; it's got the pull-down stairs. I'm 240 pounds, mind you; I wasn't as scared of the attic as I was that rickety-ass ladder. We got up there and searched around the attic. It was empty; there was nothing he could have cut himself on, but there was a milk crate over in the corner with papers on it. I went over, took the papers, and went downstairs. I looked through them, and some were unimportant. Two, however, stood out. One was a hand-sewing of a church design. The second was page two of a letter about reasons why this church was to be built. Nothing too strange was in this letter, so I just put them to the side and went on with my hangover.

I had two pit bulls at the time named Mia and Dozer. Shortly after I discovered the papers, they decided to rip them apart. That's when shit hit the fan.

Instantly, I noticed a change in atmosphere. The house felt heavy, ominous, and just all around wrong. The first night the activity started, my girlfriend and I were on the couch watching the Boobtube. Suddenly, we heard what sounded like someone jumping as high as they could then slamming their feet onto the ceiling. This scared the crap out of us. Then we heard stuff dragging across the floor, heavy like furniture.

My girlfriend looked at me. "Maybe it's a raccoon." I gave that look, like, *really??* "That's a big damn raccoon, and is he moving in? If so, he's paying rent," I said. This went on for a few weeks, sometimes two nights in a row, then would stop for a night or two. Then I started noticing weird occurrences, things missing or moved. We would find them later in random spots. Just unexplained events.

I'm pretty into the paranormal. I was part of a ghost hunting crew in Georgia, and I've had these types of events my entire life, so I thought to myself, "Great, I live in another haunted house."

After about two months there, things got progressively worse. My girlfriend and I started fighting more. I became more aggressive, more angry. It's like my personality shifted. I wasn't sleeping well. I would wake up to slams, things being thrown in the kitchen, and unexplained voices.

One night, we had another party with several friends, and we all had left to get some booze. When we got back, I went into the bathroom while everyone bee-lined for the living room. I did my business and when I came back into the living room, everyone was staring at my TV, which was off. I asked, "What the hell are you freaks doing?"

My girlfriend said to me, "Jesse, there are little kids' handprints all over your screen." Sure enough, there they were covering my screen, probably the size of a five- or six-year-old's hands. My daughter at the time was eight months old. It sure wasn't her. I cleaned off the TV and tried to have a good night, thinking I'd just ignore it until I could sort it out. Well, that blew up in my face like a damn grenade.

Two weeks later, I was leaving for Fort Wayne and had forgotten something. I ran up the stairs to get it. I headed to the bathroom and as I entered, I heard what sounded like a little kid running across my kitchen floor, giggling. I wasn't about to stick around. I grabbed my stuff and double-timed it out. Never spoke of it to my girl.

At about the four- or five-month mark of my living in this house, it started to get darker. I was changing. I'd closed myself off. I became really mean and threatening to my girlfriend. She said I was saying horrible things to her in my sleep, yelling at her, and calling her nasty names. I've never been like that, and since I left the house, I never have been again.

One night, I had a buddy stay over. We decided to stay up and play some video games and drink; normal twenty-four-year-old stuff. We finally got tired and decided to hit the rack. I slept on the couch, him on the floor. I was almost out when all of a sudden, he jumped up screaming like he was being attacked. It scared the crap out of me. I asked what happened, and he said, "I was laying here and heard a deep growl above my head. I thought it was the dogs, but when I looked up, this massive black shadow was in your hallway. I'm out, dude." He left at 3 a.m. and went home.

At this point I was so used to it, I just went to sleep. Well, a few nights later, I was laying on the floor watching TV. When I heard the growling, I jumped up, and at this point, I was pissed. I started screaming, "Show yourself!" and calling it all sorts of names. I got what I wished for. Up to this day, it still haunts me. I heard a noise coming from my daughter's room. I ran in there, and standing over my daughter's crib I found this massive black form. Luckily, my daughter wasn't there; she was at her mom's.

I was frozen. I had been dealing with the para-normal a long time. Never had I experienced anything like this. Suddenly, it just disappeared. I feel like showed itself in that room to say, "Keep taunting me, and I'll show you what I can do." A week later, I moved back to Fort Wayne, never to be plagued by this again.

# FOOTSTEPS AT THE IN-LAWS'

Is it better to understand the reason for a haunting, or is one better off not knowing why the dead have returned to make themselves known? That's the question we're left with after hearing this story.

Often when we hear a ghost story, there seems to be some rhyme or reason for the haunting to occur. One can sometimes conclude that it's a deceased relative coming back with a message, or possibly a former resident still inhabiting the place they called home. In some cases, it's a very dark entity with nothing but nefarious intentions that simply latched on to an individual without their knowledge. In this next case, though, the dead seem to make themselves known to not only the residents, but also their guests.

It also begs the question: do you let your guests know that you live in a haunted house, or do you let them discover this little secret on their own? Or do you hope and pray that it is never discovered?

Our listener shares this story about the haunting that he and his family experienced in their home.

> Tony and Jenny: a real big "How ya doin'!" from New York. I know you love practicing your accents, so try on that one. I'm an EPP (Extra Podcast Person) member and a religious listener to the show. I have not heard many stories from my neck of the woods, so I thought I'd write in about my experiences.

The story takes place in the lower Hudson Valley in a suburb twenty minutes north of New York City. Our area is steeped in lore and history going back to the founding of our nation. We are famous for stories like the headless horseman, and various Native American legends abound, but I digress.

My story begins in 2007, when I met my wife. I was a college kid in the city and my wife (girlfriend at the time) grew up relatively close to where I was going to school. I would stay over on a regular basis. I always felt uneasy when I was in the house alone, waiting for my wife to arrive back home from class or my in-laws to come back from work. I would spend most of my time downstairs in the basement, watching TV with their old terrier.

I started to realize that I would regularly hear footsteps on the first floor above me and then on the stairs to the second floor. I would have the door shut to the basement, but the distinctive sound of feet on hardwood floors was something that I could not ignore. Their dog would become agitated to the point of growling at the closed door anytime the footsteps would occur. I would constantly check or call out to see who had entered, but no one would be there. I brought this up to my wife and she admitted that she had indeed heard the footsteps. Furthermore, she felt uneasy sleeping in her old bedroom on the second floor, as she would be awoken by what she could only describe as someone stroking her hair.

My wife's family would go away for the holidays. I stayed home with my family, so I had volunteered to stay with my wife's family's dog and take him to the kennel the following day. That night was the first I had spent in the house by myself all year long. The dog and I spent quality time together, playing video games and watching TV in the basement, but I kept hearing those darn footsteps. I grew tired of the distracting footsteps and decided to go up to the first floor and stay in the living room in the front of the house with the dog.

As we sat and watched TV, the dog became upset and would regularly go to the stairs that led up to the second floor to pace back and forth. I could not shake the feeling of being watched from the second floor landing, either. At around 11 p.m., we went to sleep in my wife's old bedroom on the second floor. I shut the door and snuggled with the dog. About a half an hour later, I started to hear the footsteps again, but this time they were walking up from the first floor, past the second floor landing to the third floor. The pace and volume of the footsteps increased by the minute until it felt as if an unseen person was running up and down the stairs.

I started to get scared, and the dog stood to attention at the end of the bed and growled loudly. He would not take his focus off the closed door and the sounds coming from behind it. After about ten minutes, the footsteps went up past me to the third floor and then loudly down to the second floor landing, stopping right in front of my closed door. With the dog barking more loudly now, I made a split-second decision to burst through that closed door. I grabbed the dog and dashed through the door and down the stairs. I ran all the way out of the house and into my car parked in the driveway. I slept in the backseat of my car until dawn with the dog and a blanket I had grabbed.

After another year, my wife and I moved into the downstairs basement of the house. We created a mini studio apartment and had a new terrier puppy, as my old friend had passed away. The footsteps never ceased, but we grew to live with them. One day, we had brought some friends over and briefly left them in the basement as we went to the store to pick up some food items. When we returned, our friends promptly told us that my in-laws had arrived home because they heard the footsteps upstairs and an apparent clanging of plates. We informed them that my in-laws were actually away for the weekend and they had heard our resident spirit.

We stayed in our mini studio for three more years, and in this time, we had several very frightening experiences in the upstairs portion of the house. On a particular evening, my wife and I were going out for a night on the town, so she went to the second floor bedroom, which contained a vanity. She came briefly downstairs to retrieve a hair straightener, and when she returned upstairs I heard her let out a very loud scream. Upon running upstairs, I found her just pointing to what looked like lotion smeared all over the mirror, ceiling, and outer walls of the bedroom. The ceilings are about eight feet high and would have required my wife standing on a chair to smear the lotion. The outer walls are about seven or eight feet away from the vanity where the lotion bottle sat, perfectly intact.

Not only was there no trace of lotion anywhere on the bottle or even around it, but the bottle pump worked perfectly fine. The strangest part was the large vanity mirror, because the smears took the form of elongated hand prints complete with five fingers. I stared in amazement at the set of several prints and even tried to re-create one myself. I was able to copy the pattern on the mirror, so it must have been produced by someone's hand. We showed her parents and they simply stated that the lotion bottle must have exploded.

Several weeks later, my wife called both my father-in-law and me in an entirely frantic tone, saying that someone had broken in upstairs. She said she heard footsteps and glass breaking all over the place. As both my father-in-law and I were on our way home, we told her to lock herself in the bathroom and call 911. I arrived about five minutes later to find my wife and father-in-law looking very upset and confused. Nothing was out of place upstairs and every door and window was secure. My wife clearly looked distressed and honestly had believed her life was in danger.

The situation came to a head about two years later when my sister-in-law came to stay for a few days. She took the second floor bedroom, as we were still downstairs in the basement apartment. The morning after, she recounted that she'd awakened in the middle of the night for no apparent reason and decided to go to the bathroom. As she looked up, standing at the foot of her bed was a little girl with blond hair and pink overalls. She looked to be around eight or nine years old with a bit of a glow to her. In disbelief, my sister-in-law swiped her cellphone light back and forth in front of the girl who remained standing at the foot of her bed, staring straight at her.

My sister-in-law decided to make a break for it and slowly slid off the side of the bed to creep around to the door. As she moved around the bed, the little girl simply pivoted to watch her all the way out of the room. I never witnessed a full-body apparition myself, but I did see shadow figures on the second floor landing. My wife and I have since moved from the house into our own separate apartment, but we have never discovered the meaning or reason behind the hauntings. I'm very interested to see what you make of the situation. Thanks, and much love.

# CHAPTER 3
# ANGELS, DEMONS, & UNEXPLAINED SPIRITS

Just because it's a ghost doesn't always make it evil. Some will strongly disagree with this statement, but we firmly believe it. We've heard far too many stories of ghosts doing good for, helping, and even saving the lives of the living to find that everything we can't explain is a spawn of Lucifer whose single purpose is to steal your soul while feasting on your flesh. Stories like this are certainly intriguing and terrifying, but are far from being the ordinary experience with the dead.

There are good, bad, and seemingly neutral spirits that the living interacts with on a daily basis. At times, the purpose of these ghosts can be easily defined, while others can be extremely elusive, leaving far more questions than answers. The ghost family tree is massive and just as dysfunctional as the living family tree. There are the beloved grandmas, there are the disturbed second cousins that fall more than a few branches from the tree, and there is everything in between. What we've come to learn is that no ghost seems to be identical to another.

# FACE IN THE MIRROR

As we've learned through the course of doing the show, not all hauntings are created equal. In fact, it's relatively rare for two different people to share a similar ghostly experience with us. There are often shared elements to ghost stories, but almost every encounter is unique unto itself.

Sometimes the ghosts in the stories appear to be of somewhere other than earth and lack what we refer to as "human origins." This means the entity or ghost in the story likely never walked this planet in human form; rather, based on the actions or experiences recounted, the spirit is likely demonic or angelic in some way.

In this next story, we hear about a sleepover with two friends that began very innocently but led down a path of what can only be described as demonic jealousy. Why a powerful spirit would hold such an emotion toward a human is not exactly clear, but the hold on the individual is undeniable. Rob took the time to share his story with us.

> I tend to be skeptical about the paranormal. This is not because I don't believe that unexplainable things happen, but because most of the time what people experience can be explained by other means. I should also mention that I've always been very intuitive. I don't consider myself psychic or sensitive by any means. I don't see dead people, and I don't talk to ghosts. My gift, if you can call it that, generally has more to do with the living than the dead. I intuitively know how people

are feeling even when they try to hide it, and nine times out of ten, I can see through deception. Also, ever since I was a child, I've been able to detect the presence of evil.

I grew up in a Christian home and fortunately for me, my mother always believed me when I said I thought there was something bad or evil around. She always encouraged me and told me that God was stronger than any evil in the world, and that as long as I put my trust in him I would be okay.

Be warned: If you already have an aversion to mirrors, especially in the middle of the night, you may not want to read any further.

It was mid-summer in southeast Missouri. School was out and a friend invited me to stay the night while his parents were out of town. I was hesitant at first because I didn't know the guy very well. We had a few classes together at school and we were both video game nerds, so we had at least that much in common. He was kind of a social outcast, not by any fault of his own. He was skinny and quiet and awkward—the kind of kid that the cool kids at school liked to pick on. Needless to say, he didn't have many friends, but I liked him well enough.

I wasn't exactly a social butterfly in high school either, so I could relate. Ultimately, I didn't have anything better to do, and he had a brand-new Nintendo 64 and the new Star Fox game, so it was kind of a no-brainer. My friend lived in a trailer park that had only recently been developed, and his parents had purchased the trailer they lived in new. No one else had ever lived in it.

Almost as soon as I entered the trailer, an alarm went off in the back of my mind, and I knew that something was off. There was something about the trailer that initially gave me the creeps. The windows were all covered with tin foil, making the inside of the trailer as dark as night even in the middle of the day. I thought maybe that's where the feeling was coming from. Looking back, I wish I had listened to that alarm in my mind, but I didn't want to be rude. I ignored the feeling, pushing it as far away from my thoughts as I could.

His parents had left him some money, so we ordered pizza and enjoyed the new game for most of the evening. We were sitting in his room where the TV and N64 were hooked up. We were joking around and at one point, I grabbed a stuffed lion from the bookshelf in his room and threw it at him playfully. He caught it and placed it on his bed. Later that night, he remembered that the rabbits his father kept as pets outside needed to be fed. We went outside to feed them and when we came back into his room, the lion was back on the shelf where it had been before I threw it. I found that somewhat odd, because I left the room after he did and I would have seen if he had put it back on the shelf.

As I said before, we were the only ones there that night. I asked him about it and that's when things started to get weird. He said, "Oh, I didn't tell you? I have another friend who lives here with me. He says he's a ghost, but he's not mean or scary or anything."

I laughed at him. I wasn't trying to be mean or hurtful, but I couldn't help it. I didn't believe in ghosts. If he was offended, he didn't show it. He only went on to tell me how the ghost would even do small things for him, such as turning off the light if he didn't feel like getting up. Like I said before, I didn't know him very well and I thought that maybe he was just messing with me, so I let it go.

A few hours later, we put on a movie he had rented. I had a sleeping bag on the floor and he was in his bed. It was well past midnight by then and it wasn't long before we had both fallen asleep. I woke up at some point during the night to use the restroom. The bathroom was just around the corner from his bedroom. I flipped the light switch when I entered the bathroom but the light only came on very dimly. This was right around the time that early fluorescent light bulbs were becoming more popular, so I assumed the lights in the bathroom might be the kind that take a minute or so to warm up. I relieved myself and turned to wash my hands in the sink, and that's when I felt it.

It seems so cliché to say it, but there's no other way to describe the feeling: Someone was watching me. Not only that, it was as if the temperature were dropping rapidly in the room. A chill came over me and the hair on the back of my neck stood up. I knew all of these feelings well. They were how I always felt when evil was present.

I turned on the water and I had to bend over slightly because the sink was so low. Perhaps if my adrenaline hadn't already started to flow from the creepy feeling that filled the room, I may not have noticed that my image in the mirror didn't follow me. I froze. For a moment, I couldn't bring myself to move. I thought that maybe if I just stood there with the water running over my hands, it might wake me up and bring me back to my senses. It didn't.

I bent further and splashed some water on my face. That didn't work either. It took a moment, but I eventually mustered my courage and looked up. At first, the face looking back at me was my own, and I would have thought it was all just in my head if the image had followed my movements, but it didn't. As I watched, the face began to change. I've always been on the heavy side, and my face reflects that. I watched as my round features began to take on new, sharper ones that were not my own. The eyes changed, too. I can't really describe how they changed except to say that they became deeper. Not cavernous or dark, but somehow older and filled with the kind of depth that you might expect to see in the eyes of an old war veteran. I wanted to look away. I wanted to close my eyes and count to ten. Maybe then the image would be gone, but I was transfixed. It was as if someone were holding my head in place so I couldn't turn away. Then it spoke. "He doesn't need you. He has me, and I'm all he needs."

A familiar alarm went off in my mind again. As I said before, I'm better than most at detecting deception, and I knew in that moment that whatever this thing in the mirror was, it was lying to me. My fear slowly began to give way to anger as the pieces came together in my mind. The thing in the mirror was a predator. My friend was an extraordinarily lonely person. He was a loner, a socially awkward teenager who related more to video games than real people, and apart from me, he had no real friends. This thing had used that loneliness to attach itself to him and it had convinced him that it was just a friendly ghost who meant no harm. It began to speak again. Something about how it would never hurt him, that it was a good friend to him, but I cut it off. "I know what you are," I said. It was something that I was thinking and I didn't really mean to say it, but when I did, it stopped talking.

"You can't lie to me," I said, more boldly this time. I had never had to deal with a demon before, but in that moment, I knew that was exactly what was in the mirror in front of me. In that moment, I remembered the scripture my mother always used to quote to me when I was afraid. It was from 1 John, chapter 4. When I thought about that verse, any fear that remained was swept away and I was left with only anger at what this thing was doing to my friend. "I know what you are," I repeated, "and as long as I'm here, you can't be here." The face in the mirror began to change again and this time the image wasn't something I recognized. It certainly wasn't human. All of the features faded into deep, impenetrable shadows until all that remained were those deep, ancient eyes. It still had a face and a torso, but they were so dark that they seemed to suck in all the light around them.

"You can't make me leave!" The thing hissed at me. "Maybe not, but I speak with the authority of Christ. The Spirit of the living God dwells in me and He has authority over all things—even you. I command you, in the name of Jesus Christ, to leave this place and never return!" As soon as the words left my lips, I opened my eyes and I was back in my sleeping bag on the floor in my friend's room.

I don't think I have to tell you, but I had a hard time getting back to sleep that night. I restarted the movie that had long since ended and eventually I did drift back into a fitful slumber.

I never went back to that friend's house. We remained friends, but from that point on I insisted that we stay at my house. Now I know what you're thinking: This was a creepy story, but it was all just a dream. I have a vivid imagination, and I just made the whole thing up in my mind. I would have thought so too if that were the end of the story, but it wasn't.

I dealt with that same spirit on at least two other occasions. I wonder how many of the ghost stories that people write and call in about are demonic in nature. I know that my friend firmly believed that the entity with whom he was communicating was completely harmless. He legitimately thought it was simply another lonely spirit and that together, they were meeting a need that they mutually shared. The reality was that for whatever reason, a demonic spirit had attached itself to him. Who knows how badly that could have ended if it had continued?

# UNEXPECTED EXORCISM

For many of us, the image of an exorcism is probably something along the lines of a priest holding a crucifix, people throwing vials of holy water, and the "possessed" undergoing strange bodily contortions. As we see in the following story, apparently not all exorcisms are routine. This was a story that made us wonder about the degree to which a person can be possessed, and the ability a person may have to intervene with or break away from a demon taking over their body.

The idea of a youth group leader being able to pull off an exorcism effectively doesn't exactly play within the lines of the narrative many of us have come to understand, as you will see in this story. However, many accounts and experiences we cover on our show have made me question the "norms" or pre-conceived ideas of what is done when it comes to combating the paranormal.

Please keep in mind that we do not choose our stories to push a religious narrative of any denomination or to cast doubt on another. We take all letters and calls at face value without judgment and let you, the listener or reader, decide what you want to believe or accept in hearing the account as expressed by the author of the letter. It is up to the writer or caller to submit as accurate an account as possible. Personally, we look at this story as another unconventional experience that was a reality for a troubled young woman and the solution that she found for her troubles.

Is this the solution she found the path for everyone? Likely, no. But in her case, she claims it brought her peace from the troubles she had been experiencing. At the end of the day, that peace from torment is what most are seeking, and I'm happy she found it.

This is the story from Brittany.

This story takes place from when I was thirteen until I was seventeen. At the time of this writing, I am twenty-two and happily free from this demon that had taken over my life.

I've always been a bit sensitive to the supernatural. I've had a few paranormal things happen to me. But nothing tops when I started getting into Wicca to learn more about why I see these beings. At first, I started doing deviation and conjuring spells alone and with friends. We did everything by the books that we were told to do to make sure the spirits we encountered couldn't stay around. But it didn't work.

I would start waking up at night to find my room getting really cold, and I would get a very panicky feeling. That feeling started getting stronger and stronger, making me more uneasy. One night, I woke up to that feeling and I saw a huge, tall shadow stand at the foot of my bed. This mass blocked the light coming from the rec room where my brother was gaming. But I couldn't scream; I was in too much shock. I closed my eyes and waited for it to do something to me. When I opened them, it was gone. That was the last time I physically saw it that clearly. Other times, I would be getting ready and I would see something hiding behind the doorframe.

I told a few friends about this and how I was scared. So we asked my friend's mom, who is a Wicca practitioner (the same one who gave us instructions about how to cleanse the area after a ritual). She told us how to drive out the spirit from the house. We followed her advice, and things seemed to calm down for a couple of days.

However, one night a few weeks later, my mom and I were watching TV in the living room, and after we both feel asleep on our couch, I woke up to this feeling again. This baffled me, because it would usually leave me alone if someone else was in the same room as me. I went into a weird half trance that I really can't explain, then all of a sudden I felt an invisible force start choking me. As it was choking me, I could hear a demonic laugh in my head, and I could smell dead flesh. During this time, I could feel the presence burrow into my chest; it almost felt as if it were attempting to infect my soul. After a few seconds, it finally let go and I was free to move again.

I instantly got up and spoke to my mom, who I startled awake. Although I was in hysterics, she brushed it off and told me I just had a nightmare and to go back to sleep. But I didn't get any sleep that night, or for the next four years. After that night, I would wake up from night terrors to find myself with claw marks and bite marks on parts of my body that I couldn't even reach. I saw things lifted and dropped by the invisible force.

There was a day when my friend and I were down in my bedroom, and she jokingly went into my closet and closed the door, only to burst out of it a few seconds later saying that something attacked her.

The worst part of it was the mental things it did to me. I got very depressed and suicidal; it would implant ideas in my head such as "everyone would be happier with me dead," and "I should get it over with and kill myself." But the spirit was so clever in this; it also convinced me into thinking my thoughts were not my own, but rather its wishes for me. I almost went through with these horrible thoughts a few times, but my plans would be interrupted.

When I was seventeen, almost eighteen, I had been living with this thing for four years. I was so worn out by it that I was majorly depressed, I wasn't doing well in school, and I had turned to drugs and booze to mute the voices in my head. But I still was practicing Wicca, thinking that it would help me, and I tried every sort of cleansing thing I could. I learned later that this was the thing causing it to get worse and worse in the first place.

At this time, a Christian-based youth center had opened up in our town to help youth get off the street and to give us a safe space to hang out. None of us was happy it was Christian-based, but we went anyway because we had nothing better to do in our small town. The church's youth center had changed pastors, and he would come out and hang out with us. One night, I had a massive headache and was sitting in the kitchen while the pastor was talking to someone else about how he had become a Christian. The conversation ended, and the guy left. He started coming toward me, and I was like *oh boy, here we go*, because I hated pastors and I didn't trust them. I ended up talking to him for a bit, as he seemed to be a good man.

While talking with him, I was increasingly getting a sicker and sicker feeling in my stomach, and he noticed I was shaking. He asked me what was wrong. I told him what was going on and he said that was a sign of demonic possession.

I was baffled. Immediately the voices in my head were going crazy, screaming at me to "get out of there," and telling me that "he's mean like all the other men" and "he will hurt you." I felt like I was going to jump out of my skin. It took all my strength to stay sitting there.

He then asked me if I would like to get rid of this horrible feeling and accept Jesus. My response was something along the lines of "pssst, shhh, Jesus, nope." So I walked away that night, with no intent on ever returning.

Soon after this, the activity level increased more and more. I was being strangled and pinned down, having more night terrors, tripping down the stairs, and getting scratched and bitten. I couldn't eat anything, because I would throw it up every time. That is, until I arrived back at the church. Finally, after about two weeks, I said to myself that I was ready.

I visited the center again and met up with the pastor, not knowing what to expect. The only thing I could think of were dramatic moments from horror movies where a priest would violently drive a demon out of an unsuspecting girl. When I arrived, they only asked me to accept Jesus.

However, to get the demons out completely, I was going to have to come back when there was less commotion and other interference.

The pastor and the youth leader took me into the quiet office and started praying over me. He told me later on that my face was contorting in ways they had never seen before. I also have a recollection of involuntarily lifting up the left corner of my lip to show my teeth like a dog would. He also said that I had a hard time saying the word "Jesus" when, in my mind, I thought I was saying it fine. After their prayers, I snapped out of it. I felt like I was split in two: the demon and I were not cohabitating in my body anymore. Thank God, it was gone. The night after this experience, I had the best sleep I had in years. And I kept going to church, and I've never had a reoccurrence.

# DOG VISITORS

Often when a ghost animal is involved in a story, the identity of that animal is well known. Commonly, it is a former pet, or at least recognizable to someone close to the individual experiencing the haunting. What is very confusing about the story you're about to read is that the animals involved seem to have no relationship with the person witnessing their presence. Their purpose is also very much in question, as to whether they're good, bad, or indifferent.

Without being able to identify and examine all of the physical surroundings at the time of the experience, one must only go off the experience being recounted.

Is it all paranormal? That is for you to decide, and often a question that will linger with those who've experienced these things for the rest of their lives. Dan has the story.

The paranormal has been a part of my life from a very young age. It runs on my mom's side of the family. My sister, my mom, and I have all had dreams that came true, and we can sense when something is going on with one of us, even if we are across the country from each other. We also have an aunt a few generations back who was clairvoyant. I have had numerous experiences, but my first was by far the most bizarre and terrifying. It happened when I was seven. Prior to that, I had never had any paranormal experiences, or even an idea that the paranormal could be real. I did have nightmares very frequently from a young age, but otherwise I was a regular kid. That all changed sometime during the fall of 1997. Though the events occurred nearly twenty years ago, I still remember them vividly.

One night, I woke up from a pleasant dream I was having. My face was right at the edge of my mattress, so I could see the floor at the edge of my bed from the moment I opened my eyes. There was also a night-light right next to my bed that illuminated that whole area. Within seconds of waking up, a small white dog came out from under my bed. It moved slowly and was whimpering. I realized it was a stuffed animal that belonged to my sister that was normally in her room. I was having trouble processing what was occurring, so I wasn't really scared, just confused. I then looked up at the door to my bedroom, which was always open at night, and a golden retriever was making its way through the door over to my bed. It looked like a real dog, and though it was not transparent, it had a luminescence and glow that convinced me right away this was not a living dog. The retriever trotted over to my bed, jumped right up, and laid down at the end of it. I felt my bed move and heard the springs squeak, which made it even more startling.

I shot out of my bed, out the door, and down the stairs to the main floor where my parents slept. Since I had a lot of nightmares, my parents were used to my nighttime visits and requests to sleep in their bed. I guess they thought I was getting a bit old for that, and they tried to convince me I was only dreaming. My dad walked me back upstairs, checked under my bed, and found nothing. As he shut off the lights and headed back downstairs, I don't think I breathed. As soon as I heard the door to the main floor close, another dog appeared in my doorway. I was not waiting for it to come over to my bed this time; I darted straight out of bed and flipped on the light.

What happened next is hard to describe. It was as if the dog was a hologram, and as soon as the light came on, the image pixelated. The shape of the dog was still there, but had turned into a bunch of brightly colored squares that started to disappear one by one. I was so shocked and confused by what I was seeing that all I could do was run for my parents again.

As I entered the dark hallway, I was met halfway by—you guessed it—another dog. This one was a small dog with floppy ears and curly black fur. It was blocking my escape and started matching my movements as I went back and forth in an attempt to go around it. I noticed there was a toy near my feet, so I kicked it at the dog, which pixelated and dissipated just like the first. I ran back downstairs to my parents' room. They still didn't believe anything was going on, and led me once again to my room. My dad noticed my favorite stuffed animal, a cat, was lying on the floor of my room. He gave it back to me and said it would protect me.

When I was alone again, I braced myself, expecting the dogs to return.

They didn't.

Instead, other strange things started to happen. There were shelves mounted on the wall, and they seemingly began to fly around the room—the shelves themselves didn't move, but it was almost like the "spirits" of the shelves left the physical objects and started to fly around. There was an old TV, the kind with the dial to switch channels, sitting on a dresser at the foot of my bed. The screen and buttons appeared to be flashing bright colors, but again, I could tell it wasn't physically happening. It was more like there was an overlay of light in front of the screen and but-tons that was flashing. This was really scary, but at that point, I was just relieved the dogs hadn't come back. I decided my best option was to turn toward the wall and try to sleep.

I only woke up one time during the night. I rolled over, and saw that there was a very small Doberman Pinscher and a bunch of old fashioned toys, like jacks and blocks, lying next to my bed. As soon as I looked, they started to bounce noiselessly in slow motion toward the door and out of my room. They had the same qualities as the previous things I had seen, glowing and clearly not physically real. Again, I was just happy that was all I saw, and turned back over to go to sleep.

When I woke up again, it was light. I was confused at first because it was a school day, so my mom typically woke me up.

That's when I saw it.

My stepbrother would visit some weekends, so he had a bed across the room from me next to the door. There was a green chair from one of our play tables on top of it for some reason, and under the chair was the black dog from the hallway. It was just rolling around noiselessly underneath the seat. I laid there for a few seconds, frozen with fear. When I realized the dog was not coming after me, I sat straight up in bed. As soon as my head left the pillow, that dog disappeared. I slowly laid back down. When my cheek made contact with the pillow, the dog reappeared. I shot back up, and it disappeared again.

At that point, I got all scientific, and laid down on the floor next to my bed to see if it would reappear, but it didn't. I could have easily brushed that night off as a dream or hallucination. Honestly, nothing would have made me happier than if it was not real. It was as if this dog was purposely showing itself in the light of day so that I would know, without a shadow of a doubt, that what I experienced was real.

I went downstairs, and my mom told me I would not be going to school that day as I had hardly slept. She still wouldn't listen to me, and insisted that it was my imagination, or some kind of dream. I tried to continue as normal, but knew this temporary peace would be shattered when night fell. That evening and countless ones that followed would be spent gripped by fear and anxiety that the dogs would return. Thankfully, they never have.

Even though they never came back, they did continue to haunt me in my dreams. My nightmares became entirely dog focused, and any dream even containing a dog became a nightmare. I had one recurring nightmare about the black dog from the hallway for more than a decade after it happened.

The dream always goes like this: I wake up in my bedroom or a familiar setting. It could be any bedroom I had up until that point. As soon as I wake up, I know the black dog is there. I can't exactly see it, but I know where it is and that it's coming. I hear a soft panting followed by a shrill scream, and then I wake up. Sometimes it's just that bit, other times I would have a whole dream with that as the ending. The dreams decreased in occurrence as I grew older, and they finally stopped sometime after I turned eighteen.

The summer following the incident, my parents announced that we were moving. It was in the same town, but in a more rural area. I continued to have paranormal experiences, including seeing ghosts, but never anything like what I saw that night. As a young adult, I discovered I am sensitive to energy and am an empath. It is rather mild and nearly shuts off when I am in work mode or stressed. With this new perspective, I have spent a lot of time thinking about that night and its significance. There must be some reason the dogs appeared to me out of nowhere, never to be seen again. It could have been energy left behind in the house (it was over one hundred years old), but it doesn't make sense that it was the only thing anyone ever experienced in the years we lived there. I can't help but think the dogs were some sort of spirit animal that for whatever reason decided to visit me that night. Naturally, I was terrified, but the dogs never really did anything threatening.

I wonder now if they were just trying to get my attention. I wonder what would have happened if I had responded with curiosity instead of fear. What course would my life have taken? Would I have full-blown psychic abilities instead of sensitivity? I think I created some sort of block on my "abilities" that night because I just couldn't cope with it. It scarred me very deeply, and to have everyone tell me it wasn't real just made it worse. Since these realizations, I have tried to heal from the experience to remove any blocks. I even went as far as to write an open letter to the spirits saying how I was not ready at the time, but now understood they meant me no harm. I asked them to remove the block and return if that was necessary, but nothing seemed to change. The dogs still didn't return.

Truly, I'm grateful. I'd like to think I'm ready to face them, but the thought still terrifies me to this day. I don't think about it much anymore, but writing this now, I know I'll have dogs on the brain while trying to sleep tonight. Of all the ghost stories I've heard throughout the years, nothing is even akin to this. I recently started listening to your show, and love what you guys are doing! With all my experiences, sharing ghost stories is very therapeutic. I'm glad to see things have changed, and that people are more open to the idea of the paranormal. If my parents had been more open, I imagine things would be very different for me today.

# CHAPTER 4
# THE GRAVEYARD SHIFT

It's one thing to have a haunted home, where you can choose to keep your ghostly encounters to yourself. It's a whole other world of confusion and difficulty when your workplace is the home of choice for the undead. What can be even more surprising are the businesses that ghosts seem to choose to haunt.

Many of us go back the preconceived notion of a haunted funeral home, church, or dangerous factory where multiple accidents have taken place. The reality, however, is that just like homes, ghosts do not discriminate as to where they haunt. Some seem to haunt for the love of a job they once had; some appear to be stuck in place, others try to lend a helping hand, and some would be an HR nightmare if caught in the act of their haunts.

The next time you feel you have a boring job, ask yourself, would it be better to have a ghost in the workplace?

## SECURING THE DEAD

There are many careers in this world that involve emotionally charged situations. While one may simply be there to provide care, those being cared for could be in for the fight of their lives.

Working in the medical field, and specifically working in buildings and facilities that have a history of trauma surrounding them, can be troubling to some. Even if the traumatic events happened long ago, the imprint that was left on the atmosphere can still be felt today. Sometimes that imprint is nothing more than a residual energy, but sometimes it is much more.

Can repeated and concentrated negative acts combine to form a conscious entity? In our next story, this is a question that we are left to contemplate. Here is the story from our listener Jesus:

> This is an account of the paranormal events that took place where I was once employed.
>
> I worked at a supportive living center for developmentally disabled individuals. This facility has been in existence since the early 1900s, and by the 1920s they started accepting people with developmental disabilities, and it has been that way ever sense.
>
> Now anyone familiar with psychiatric treatment, especially the type performed in the early 1900s, knows that types of treatment weren't always the most

"enlightened" or ethical. These treatments, combined with outbreaks of flu, measles, and small pox, provided an atmosphere ripe for the type of energy that would cause someone to linger in this world.

This job was my very first foray into such a field, and therefore I had entered the job with some trepidation. The more comfortable I became with my job, the more comfortable I became with my coworkers. Naturally, I shared with them my love for the paranormal. Instead of being greeted by skepticism, I was greeted with several stories and personal accounts that many of the workers there had experienced in their time employed at the facility.

When I started my job, I was put on the 6 a.m. to 2 p.m. shift. During my two-and-a-half years working those hours, I did not have a single experience.

A few years into my employment, the location I worked in merged with another, and I was required to relocate to another home facility. I was moved to the juvenile care home and placed on the 10 p.m. to 6 a.m. shift. The change in hours was brutal, but I thought that if I was going to experience anything at this facility, the night shift was going to be where it would happen.

There was one story in particular that I was eager to check out. The rumor was that there was a series of tunnels that connected certain buildings—tunnels that were no longer in use because their original use would not fly in today's world. I learned of the entrance to the tunnels and quickly found that they were locked. This should've been obvious, as we had several residents that walked around the facility, and we would not want them getting in there. Not one to give up, I asked security if there was any way that I could get into the tunnels, just for a peek. I was denied, but was not sent away empty handed.

One of the security officers shared with me what their original use was. According to him, these tunnels were used to house the more dangerous individuals; the guards would shackle the patients to the walls in the tunnels and leave them there to break their spirits. He also told me that the shackles were still on the walls and security was ordered not to let anyone into them.

It did not stop there. He said that from the other side of the locked doors, officers would often hear knocks and scratches when they were making sure the doors were still secured.

I left disappointed, but also satisfied with the information I had been given.

When I started on my shift at the new home, everything went pretty smoothly. I had hoped for more action, and was a little let down that what I thought would be a sure bet turned out to be a flop. It was about a month in when things started to pick up.

Now, it is important to note that this building had been closed until they had restaffed it, right when I changed locations. Allegedly, all the original staff that had worked this place had been let go due to complaints of abuse, and the Department of Justice had closed the first juvenile facility. I was one of the first to stay the night in that location for several years, and due to the old staff being gone, I could not get any interesting stories.

On this night in particular, the phone rang, and when I answered it, I was greeted by a camera monitor on the other end who asked me if all of our boys were in their rooms sleeping. I knew the answer was yes, but to placate the camera monitor, I did a quick head count and they were all indeed in their rooms. I asked the monitor why they wanted to know. They told me that they had seen someone walking around the living room on the camera but could not tell who they were.

I had them stay on the line as I went up front to the living room to check it out. It could've been a resident of another home, or maybe even someone who had broken in. But as the safety of the residents was our primary concern, I had to go check. I was a bit hesitant, as I had personally locked the doors to the home upon arriving, but just in case, I went and checked them all. Thankfully, they were secured, and there was no one to be found in the living room.

Satisfied with my search but still unnerved by what they had seen, the camera monitor opted just to leave it be, and I agreed.

Aside from me, there were two other staff members working the shift. Our duties mainly consisted of making sure the residents were monitored during the night, as some were prone to seizures and other medical issues. We were also in charge of doing the laundry and general cleaning of the home, but for the most part, we sat in the hallway at night to be close to the residents.

From the lobby, you could see the living room. We would often see a shadow walk from one side of the living room to the other, but it was usually out of the periphery and we could never really get a good look at it. No one admitted to this until another staff member who was working an overtime shift mentioned it, and it turned out we had all seen that shadow at some point during our shifts.

Pretty tame, I'll admit, but still rather disturbing, considering there was no one else in the home but us.

Another thing we all came to experience was footsteps.

The first time I heard them, I was in the staff bathroom doing my business. I heard footsteps right outside of the door, like someone was waiting for me to finish using the bathroom. I walked out and expected to see one of my coworkers but was greeted by no one, which was odd considering that I had not heard the footsteps leave. I walked to the back where the others were and asked if anyone had walked up to the front, and both vehemently denied doing so. By this time, we were all familiar with the shadowy figure walking in the living room so I did not hesitate to share what I had just experienced. One of my colleagues stated that the same thing had happened to her; out of the ordinary, yes, but still rather benign as far as paranormal activity goes. We came to accept these things; they happened on a nightly basis and although they were a bit freaky, they did not scare us all that much. Had it stayed that way, we would've been satisfied, but this would not have been a good experience now, would it?

One night while sitting and listening to your podcast, I became thirsty. Deciding to save my energy drink for later, as I had a sixteen-hour shift waiting for me that day, I decided that I would drink some water. I made my way into the living room and began to head toward the kitchen, and I'll admit that I was startled by our lights, which come on automatically when they detect movement.

We had an ice machine that also dispensed water in the kitchen. The kitchen had to remain locked, as most of our residents are on strict diets and are not allowed to have access to foods at their leisure. This is generally due to weight issues and things like disabilities. I reached for the doorknob but before I could take hold of it, the knob began to rattle.

I quickly recognized this as someone jiggling the doorknob from the other side. I took a step back and watched as the doorknob continued to jiggle. Still, I was undaunted, so I reached for the doorknob once more but stopped when I noticed something. From under the door, you could see feet, or the shadows of feet, as if someone were on the other side of the door. When I noticed it the jiggling of the doorknob stopped.

I stood quietly, afraid to make a move; it seemed whatever was on the other side of that door was well aware that I had taken notice of it. What felt like an eternity passed as I stood frozen. The thing on the other side of the door did not move either. I was not eager to break this stalemate, but I also wasn't eager to stay where I was. I summoned my courage, turned, and walked rather quickly back toward the hallway where I would be among my coworkers.

I must've been obviously freaked out, because my coworkers took notice. They asked what was the matter, though they had some idea as to the cause of my fear.

I explained to them what I had just experienced and was met with complete acceptance. Not only that, but one of my coworkers also shared a similar experience. It turns out that he, too, had witnessed the doorknob jiggling, but he didn't stick around long enough to see the cause. I was shaken up, but found comfort among other people. That comfort did not last long.

We were all sitting and doing our own thing after we ran out of topics to speak of, as we were all different types of personalities with little in common. It was then that a loud scream broke the silence.

I was sitting in the back of the hallway and as I had headphones on, I assumed that the scream was part of the podcast I was listening to. It was then that one of my colleagues walked to the back of the hallway to get my attention. They asked if I had heard the scream, and I nodded my head. From where I sat, it sounded as if it had come from the front of the building, but to them, it sounded as if it had come from the back. The first step that needed to be taken was to ensure that the residents were okay. A quick room check showed me that they were all sleeping soundly, not so much as a peep. I investigated the back of the building: I found nothing.

I then investigated the front of the home and again, I was greeted by nothingness. I did not feel satisfied with my search and decided to check in a few extra places where only employees had access. I reached for my keys and made my way to the laundry room.

I unlocked the laundry room door and turned the knob. I instantly felt as if someone on the other side of the door was holding on to the doorknob, which prevented me from entering the room. Now I'm not going to sit here and say that I'm a strong guy, but I've got a fair amount of strength. Still, no matter how hard I pushed on the door, I could not get through. I pushed harder and harder; I don't know why I was so insistent on getting inside, but I just felt like I had to. The harder I pushed, the more I was resisted. It was quite frustrating. I kept pushing until finally the force on the other side of the door pulled away, and I barreled through the door and onto the ground. I picked myself up off the ground and looked around to see that the laundry room was empty.

Irritated and a bit scared, I turned to make my way out of the laundry room. As I took hold of the knob, I heard a very clear "Hey!" in my ear. When I turned to look behind me out of instinct, I was met by nothing except a laugh that was once again directly in my ear. I booked it out of the laundry room and decided to put an end to my search. I reported my findings to my coworkers and we spent the rest of the night on edge, waiting for something else to happen which, fortunately for us, never did.

Then came the night that things took a turn.

This night was unusually quiet. Everyone seemed to be rather sedated, and that was not often the case. Usually, a resident would linger around for some staff attention, but on this night, they were all asleep in their rooms. The night proceeded like it was supposed to. We did our room checks, laundry, and cleaning without a single incident. It was about 3 a.m. when one of my coworkers started complaining about the music she heard from the room she was sitting outside of. I reminded her that the resident in that room had several toys that produced sounds and music and that was most likely what she was hearing. She accepted that and a few minutes passed by. Then she hopped out of her seat; something had startled her.

She waved me over and explained to me that she had seen something walk across the windows in the resident's room; in fact, the curtains were still in motion when I looked inside. This was the first time anyone had seen that shadow figure in a resident's room or in the hall. I tried to write this off, as this resident in particular had a habit of waking up in the middle of the night and pacing back and forth throughout his room. This would've been all well and good, but the resident was in a deep sleep.

When I entered the room, I also heard the music. It sounded like circus music but distorted, like it was coming from a dying toy. I looked all around for the source of the sound but could not find anything, nor did I have any knowledge that he had a toy that made that noise. Everyone became unnerved, and as the leader, I had to remain strong. I told her that I would switch seats with her and elected to sit in front of that resident's room. The music continued to play and, with each note of the song, I began to lose my cool.

I put my headphones back on to listen to other people's ghost stories, which seemed counterproductive as I was currently living one of my own. This did not help drown out the music, despite how loud I turned my volume up.

Now the way we sat was with our backs to the doorway; this was mainly because no one liked facing the rooms, as you could see out of the windows. I began to feel like I was being stared at, which is a feeling I detest. I tried to ignore it, thinking it was just para- noia from listening to the stories and from the activity going on around us. I turned to look to see just what was staring at me and again I was greeted by nothing, though I did notice that the curtains were once again swaying, as if something had brushed against them.

Eventually, I had to get up and go to the bathroom. I informed my coworker and had her sit in my seat, because this resident needed an employee's attention when he first woke up, so someone had to be close at all times. I went to the bathroom, and when I came back into the hallway, my coworker was not in her seat. Instead, I found her in the room staring out the window. The music was still playing, but now there was a heavy feeling of oppression that had taken hold of the place. I called out to her, but there was no reply.

I moved toward her and tapped her on the back, and she quickly turned to face me, a look of anxiousness on her face. She pointed out the window to what appeared to be a white light that was making its way down the street toward our building.

I stood stunned as we watched the light. It was a single bright light, so the chance that it could've been a car was out of the question. It seemed far away, but it was slowly making its way toward us. We did not say a word, but there was clearly a feeling of terror that had washed over us. Despite this, we could not move from our spots; we were glued as if attracted to this white light. It grew closer and closer, and eventually we could begin to make out a form in the shape of a person. Arms, legs, and head were clearly visible, but it was still too far away to make out any other features. I wished it had stayed that way.

It had come very close at this point, almost directly across the street from us. We could not believe what we were seeing. Within this light was a man, who in his normal appearance was more frightening than anything I have seen to this date. He seemed so average that he was more like an impersonation of what someone would think a person would be, as a vague description that someone would give to someone who had never seen a human being. The one thing about him that wasn't average was his height. He was short, not by conventional standards either. He was no larger than three feet high, or at least that is what I'd estimate. At first, I thought it might've been a little person; a few had called this facility home over the years. The thing was that it was perfectly proportioned; nothing looked out of place. He seemed like a perfectly molded person, only three feet in height. Like a doll crafted to perfect human specifications.

He strode along the street with an arrogant gait, his stride deliberate and confident. He wore what appeared to be jeans and a T-shirt, though his clothing was almost as nondescript as he was. As he drew closer, we could see the smirk on his lips; it was as if he owned the night and he knew it. It radiated evil, or at least what I assume evil feels like.

I've experienced quite a few things in my life from witchcraft to spirits and have never felt anything that felt like that. It was suffocating; you could feel it all around you. As it turned to move toward the home we noticed its most disturbing feature: no eyes. It was not like its eyes had been removed, but there were simply no sockets, nowhere for an eye to be. Instead, there were hollow pits of abyssal blackness that seemed to pull you into them. My colleague fainted at this point, dropping to the ground in a heap from fright. I kept watching as the little man walked past our facility. It turned its head and I quickly ducked down, not wanting it to see me. I felt like something bad would happen if it did. My heart raced and I stayed hidden in the room, kneeling down next to my fallen colleague. I peeked over the window and saw that the being continued to walk forward, toward the infirmary, where it disappeared. I took in a deep breath and waited for a few moments before waking my coworker. She did not want to talk about what we had seen; in fact, after that night, she quit her job.

I did not see that thing again after that night, but some strange things happened afterward.

Three homes went into quarantine after an outbreak of the flu. Two residents died, one in his sleep and the other out of the blue. Now it is not strange for residents to die; we do have several seniors with a host of health issues. However, the two that died were relatively young and the investigations, which have to be done anytime someone dies simply to dismiss the possibility of wrongdoing, were inconclusive as to what caused the death. Now these could be coincidences for sure, but the timing was just strange.

The final piece to this incident came several months later. I had switched over to the morning shift, which was unrelated to the paranormal stuff. I had a ghost-hunting app on my phone that I was messing around with, testing it on our home. I walked out of the facility and to the sidewalk. When using the spirit box feature, I got a voice that said "the little man," followed by what sounded like the same music from the resident's room. I do not know what that thing was, but I do know that it was evil.

There was much evil done at this facility in the name of medical advancement, a lot of pain and suffering. I believe whole-heartedly that these things can imprint themselves upon a building or even the land on which these events occurred. Could it have been that this thing was born of all the negativity of this place, or could it be that this thing feeds on or causes the adverse events that occurred there?

People change when they take this job. I do not know if it is because of the environment or something more sinister. Depression is pretty common; there have also been some outbursts of anger and people behaving out of character. The thing I learned through all this is that there is evil in this world, things that tug on the most primal of fears, fears that have dwelt within the hearts of man since the start of time.

# LONG-TERM EDUCATION

For most, college is a time of firsts, but for some it is a time of lasts. Students can leave college in a cap and a gown, or in a trip to the ER with the knowledge that they are not really invincible, or they can choose to leave and return home due to being overwhelmed with emotion and pressure. Sadly, they don't always leave among the living. The energy expelled during these events must go somewhere, but it never truly leaves.

But where does it go? Who does it follow? What does it inhabit? As we learn in so many stories from universities all over the world, there is no simple answer to these questions.

In this story, we learn about an energy that lingers around a college campus, with a habit of toying with the employees charged with keep the grounds safe and sanitary. Our friend Green shares this story:

This is a story about experiences at a college I worked at, a college located in what some would call an old college town. It straddles the line between stuck in the turn of the century and begrudgingly modern, but in no fascinating way. The atmosphere and tendencies of the locals seem to fit that description, too. The college, for its part, does well at trying to be an entity unto itself in the sleepy town. However, for all its efforts, the very raw and visceral emotions that arise at the college seem to trap more than one school's fair share of specters, which appear to wait in the night. To me, it always made sense that the school would be haunted.

The college is not merely a building, but rather a nexus. A nexus for which new life events can happen for people who, just months ago, were considered children, but are now adults. And young adults feel on such deep levels, and see the world in such bright prisms of possibilities for themselves and the world around them, that it only stands to reason that high energy would get soaked up into the limestone foundations and porous walls in which these people live. So it fits that, with nearly fifty years of a quickly changing world under its belt, the school is ripe with energy and activity.

I work in the main campus building, one of the oldest and busiest on campus. Most of the general education classes take place in this building from 7 a.m. until nearly 10 p.m., and there is a relatively new theater in my building that was renovated about six years ago. The library, student adviser offices, professors' offices, suites, and computer labs are scattered throughout the building. It can easily take on the feeling of a labyrinth for the unfamiliar.

When I started working for the college at the top of the year, I did not encounter anything ghostly; just picked up on energies. They are, as you can suspect, chaotic in their inconsistencies. However, by the spring of that year, I started hearing usually female voices conversing indistinctly, way after closing. Sometimes, in my peripheral vision, I would see people. However, my first full-bodied apparition was encountered during spring break, when we were assigned to give the restrooms the most thorough and backbreaking cleaning imaginable.

Innumerable gallons of water are used in this process, and we exert a notable amount of physical energy. My colleague on this assignment was getting a fresh start on the restroom next to the one I was finishing up. By this time, the campus was closed to everyone. While cleaning one of the stalls, I saw a women who could have stepped right out of the late '70s or very early '80s walk past the doorway. She had almost strawberry blond hair in the Farrah Fawcett style. She wore a silk rainbow top and high-waisted turquoise pants. She did not acknowledge my presence in any way, just merely walked. I heard the clicking of her heels as she walked by. A door leading to the back parking lot sits right next to this restroom and I heard to that door open. I went to make sure the door latched, as we were closed, and I saw neither her nor any vehicle drive off.

In my gut, I knew she was a ghost. Sometime later, my colleague and I were splitting up the restrooms again, but for routine cleaning. I had the women's, and he had the men's. He walked in looking perturbed. He wasn't one to get too excited about anything, but on that day, he looked angry with me. He asked me what I wanted. I looked at him blankly, and a little perturbed myself for being torn away from my task, for presumably, a game.

I responded, "Nothing, why do you ask?" His face contorted inquisitively; he said, "You didn't bang on the walls?"

The restrooms share a wall for plumbing. I replied, "No. Are you messing with me?" As serious as he could, he implored that he thought I was messing with him and wanted me either to say what I wanted or not to try to spook him. I insisted to the contrary that I was not and had not tried to frighten him.

Our shift runs from 3 p.m. to midnight, and the cleaning for the restrooms is often the very last part of the shift, so it is not uncommon for us to be in the thick of it around 11 p.m. And it seems this would be a bit of a theme in the coming years. Later that year, an area fair was taking place. It was the last day or two before closing. The college's parking lot runs to the state fairgrounds. This often causes confusion and misunderstandings with the out-of-town fair-goers, who associate our campus with the event itself. We are completely separate. But as a result, by 5 p.m., we sometimes lock the doors to keep the drunks and campers from stumbling into the building. They tend to have a bad habit of spreading all kinds of bodily fluids in the bathrooms.

On this particular night, I was making my rounds at about 11 p.m. to double-check all the doors and make sure they were locked and that nobody had wondered into the building. One of the entryways is for handi-capped accessibility. This door is adjacent to the rear entrance of the black box theater double doors. There is a thin strip of space between the double doors that allows some light to shine through. Walking past them to check this handicapped entrance, I noticed nothing out of the ordinary, but as I casually walked past after confirming the entrance was locked, I saw that the lights in the black box were on. My colleague liked trying to spook me; I assumed this was a poor prank on his part.

I opened the doors and saw the front entrance of the theater shutting lazily. I ran to the other side, thinking I would be able to catch him and rub in how weak his effort was. The front entrance is attached to a narrow corridor that has the benefactors' names on one wall and a montage of forty years of student actors on the other. The entrance door to this hall was shut. The light was on, however. I ran and burst through the door, suspecting my colleague would be on the other side waiting to yell, "BOO!" He wasn't there.

I looked left, nobody. I looked right, nobody. I walked to the back end of the building where the bath-rooms are, and he was standing at the back entrance thoroughly engrossed in a conversation with an acquaintance of his.

About a year later, going into autumn, we were once again cleaning these restrooms and stopped to take a break. Outside of the women's restroom, we heard something like a moaning come from inside. We both heard it. I knocked on the door. "Custodian. Anyone in here?" Silence. Nobody was there.

By spring of that next year, the weird noises and peripheral forms had become white noise to me. But on three occasions this year, some heavier activity happened that spooked me, the culmination of which was just this past week.

My colleague was replaced with an older gentleman in spring, and he was far less sociable. But to his credit, he'd do the work you asked him to do. And as sure as spring came, we had been invited to detail the restrooms once more.

Now, my new colleague wore this brown pair of sketcher shoes and blue jeans. Always. I was scrubbing the tile in the stalls and around the urinals while I had him siphoning the water and suds from the disinfectant on the floor. While cleaning in a stall, I saw his feet and his jeans beneath the stall wall. But he wasn't siphoning. To be fair, the man didn't always play with a full deck, and I thought to myself, "You have got to be kidding me. Is he taking a leak right now?" Despite having had all the ghostly activity in that building, I still believed he was pissing on my clean floor and urinals before I thought anything else. I rounded the corner to reprimand him. To my surprise, he wasn't even in the restroom.

I was alone.

Thankfully, for me, by summer, he felt he was better off retired than trucking along as a custodian. So, I got a new colleague. She was an immigrant from Ukraine. She and I kicked it off real good and worked together most of the time. On occasion, we would meander into the library to have either a much-needed coffee break or water break. Now, the library has its own set of issues. But the one thing I can say that raises my hair is the theft detection system the library uses. It senses a magnetic chip all the books have in them. If the book, movie, game, or anything else the library offers has not been properly checked out, the sensors by the three entrances will go off. It does not have a built-in testing system. It cannot be controlled from the circulation desk. It is very basic equipment, and it is reactionary. You walk through with the magnet, and it buzzes at you.

On one particular evening—yes, once again around 11 p.m.—the alarm sounded at us. My colleague and I were talking about your podcast, *Real Ghost Stories Online*.

She jumped.

She asked what made that noise. I explained it to her. I said that it's strange how it happens but not to worry about it. Joking, I added, "It's probably our ghost!" Without fail, the buzzer went off immediately.

She latched hold of my arm, and we shuffled off. The ultimate, however, was this week's event.

She was in the men's restroom cleaning, while I was by the water fountain, cleaning and polishing it. I hear her talking and laughing, but I'm not paying much attention. I figure she is on the phone with one of her children. No big deal. Minutes later she yells, "Oh hush!" By about this point, I am finished with the water fountain, and go to the restroom where she is to inquire whom she was speaking with.

She wasn't on her phone.

She gave me a strange smile and somewhat timid look and said, "Don't mess with me. I'm not in the mood to be scared." I looked equally perplexed now. I retort, "I don't know what you are talking about. I heard you talking and laughing. I figured you were on your phone." In kind, she responded, "No ... I was telling you about how Zach scared me last week and made me scream. So I was laughing about it while retelling you."

Shocked now, I said "I never asked you about that. I was cleaning the water fountain."

She looked very unnerved. She said, "You were speaking to me from around the corner. You asked me about how I got scared last week. Why are you trying to frighten me now?" I looked her in the eyes and promised, "I love joking with you. But I am telling you, I wasn't speaking at all."

So it seemed, a disembodied voice communicated with my colleague using my voice somehow. She was shaken to the core, and didn't go anywhere without me the rest of the week!

# BEATRICE IN THE WINDOW

The connection that good caregivers share with our elders in their final years can be incredibly strong. Raw and honest emotion is shared, along with realizations about life and our purpose. It's no wonder, then, that once the cared-for individual passes on, they would want to give a final message to those who were around for their final days, especially because very often, those final moments are hard to predict.

In this story, one such caregiver shares her account of working and caring for an elderly woman in her final stretch of life, and the visit she received from the afterlife. Ellie writes to us:

> When I was working at a retirement home as a house-keeper between my junior and senior years of college in 2013, I came to work one day to find a long blue van parked near the building that I had been assigned to. It looked like a commercial van, discreet, with no company logos or anything on the side. I had never seen it there before, so I took a peek inside.
>
> There was a cot or gurney in the back with a knitted blanket and a pillow. I knew right away what it was there for. I walked into the main building so I could get my supply cart and clock in for the day. It was about 6:45 a.m.
>
> Just to start conversation, I asked my boss about it. "Hey Teresa, what's the van all about?"

"Oh, Beatrice passed away. They're here to pick up her body and take her to the morgue," my boss replied in a casual tone. In a retirement home, death is pretty much the next step for many of the residents. From my earlier nursing home experiences as a dietary aide, I was no stranger to the pattern. It seemed as though at least three residents passed each month, though I never experienced anything mysterious at the previous retirement home, where I'd worked for almost two years.

On this particular day, my boss decided that we needed to do some floor care in the main building and clean out another room in the independent living building to get it move-in ready, but first, she wanted to help me get all my rooms done. She was an awesome boss because she had only recently become a supervisor. I also knew her from previous assignments.

We ended up going through the door on the northwest side of the main building so we wouldn't be in the way of the Beatrice's room, which was the last one on the northeastern side. After we got our supplies together, my supervisor and I followed the pathway between the main building and the north side of my building. It was about the length of a short neighborhood block.

We started cleaning rooms along west hallway. While we were making our way to another room, all the lights in that hallway went dim for just a second, then got really bright before going back to normal. There were between six and eight individual lights down the ceiling of the hallway. I didn't think anything of it, but in hindsight, it's really weird that it happened, given what we were about to experience. I remember my supervisor made a comment about how she was going to talk to maintenance because in all the time she worked in that building, which had been years, that had never happened before.

After some time passed and we'd cleaned a few rooms, we were making out way back to the main building to get our floor care supplies. Just two separate buffers—one for carpet, and one for hard linoleum, to give it that spit shine.

I was walking behind her pushing the cart, and she was rolling the vacuum. As I was pushing my cart, I noticed that the blue van was gone. I glance over to the window where Beatrice's room was. To my surprise, *I saw her looking out the window!* She was literally looking over toward us, very confused. I saw her maybe for about two seconds. I looked at my boss, then at the window again, and she was gone.

"Uh, Teresa, is Beatrice still here?" I already knew the answer.

"No, they took her, see, the van is gone."

"So, why the hell did I just see Beatrice in the window?!"

"You saw her too?"

Now, there is *no* flipping way that Beatrice would have been at the window. On top of the fact that she was now *dead*, when I had started working there for the summer, she was already declining in health and was bedridden. I had cleaned her room maybe three times (we cleaned each resident's room weekly). By the fourth week, her family was visiting her and saying their goodbyes, so I was instructed not to clean her room. I avoided her room for about two weeks before the ominous blue van showed up.

The times that I did clean her room, I remember her and her sunken light eyes looking at me, almost helpless, from her throne of a bed. She wasn't scary or anything, just old. There was no way in hell she would have been able to get up. What makes this particularly interesting is that the last time I did clean her room, she was wearing a purple nightgown. When I saw her in the window, she was wearing the same color nightgown.

I know that there's a myth, I guess you'd call it, about opening windows to let out the dead. Well, the windows in this retirement home were large, but only the bottom third could be opened. I think she was confused because she was standing up. She looked real. It was like she literally got up out of bed and decided to look through the window. I will never forget that moment.

I enjoy your guys' show very much and will soon become an EPP at ghostpodcast.com. I love listening to the podcast while I'm at work. I have other stories that I'd be happy to share. I'll be writing again soon!

# CHAPTER 5
# HALLOWED GROUND

Just because you've exited through the door of a haunted building doesn't mean you are free from ghosts. In fact, stories of haunted woods, streets, paths, or you-name-it outdoor areas are just as familiar as haunted homes or businesses. Outdoor hauntings can sometimes be even more confusing, as the ghosts that make appearances are not always in the form of a living being.

Some of the most intriguing haunt stories we've heard revolve around physical structures appearing and disappearing where they once stood. Large buildings, seen clear as any other building by the living, vanish within minutes. Are these illusions caused by some factors of nature we are unaware of, or is there a consciousness on the other side reminding us of our physical environments from times past? Either way, it seems no matter where you go, you'll never be too far from ghosts of some sort.

## FROM THE SHADOWS CAME A MAN

It's hard not to smile when thinking back to our younger days of venturing out to explore a haunted area without a care.

We were on a mission for adventure. The prospect of seeing something paranormal crossed our minds, but this possibility seemed about as likely as being stopped at a railroad crossing for a man in a sleigh pulled by flying reindeer.

Many of us who went out searching for ghosts probably felt the same way. We desperately wanted to experience something but kept calm, knowing that it was not going to be a likely outcome. The most any of us ever experienced was a jackass friend sneaking up from behind some bushes when no one was paying attention.

That is not the case in this next story about friends out for a night of fright. As they came upon an abandoned building near a cemetery (the perfect setting for a ghost story, right?), they learned, very quickly, that an innocent adventure could turn into a life-changing experience. It made them question everything they had come to believe and understand about the relationship between the existence of the living and the dead.

This story has not made us stop seeking out abandoned places and documenting their beauty on film, but it has made us more cautious about the shadows we see. It's forced us think twice about whether that shadow in the corner should be there, to evaluate the depth of darkness a shadow gives off. It may make you feel the same.

Here is the chilling experience from Sean.

I live in a rural area of Illinois, an area nestled in the armpit between Chicago and Rockford. Listening to your show has brought back many memories of unexplained occurrences that I would like to share with you. Today, I would like to tell you about my ventures down a mysterious and ominously named road in my area. The names of the people involved in this story have been changed.

Perhaps I should start with a brief rundown of this local legend. It is said that the road is haunted by a phantom truck that will appear out of nowhere and chase you out of the area. In the middle of the six-mile stretch, there is a bridge over railroad tracks, where a school bus accident supposedly occurred many years ago. Midnight thrill-seekers will stop their car, shift into neutral, and be pushed to safety by the spirits of the children lost in the horrific crash. Many other stories have been reported in the general area; ghostly apparitions wander the cemetery to the east, ominous lights dart around the woods to the west, and a witch growls and prowls everywhere in between. Strange figures appear alongside the road or within the cornfields; some say they are the victims of a brutal family murder, from which the road has received its eerie name.

This last tale, among many things, is false. In the 1930s, a man with a particularly "creepy" last name allegedly came to the area and called his settlement by that name. That's it, nothing spooky to it. And there's more burst for that bubble! There is absolutely no record of any school bus accident that took place on the bridge, or anywhere on the road for that matter. I can tell you from first-hand experience that the only thing haunting the bridge is gravity, seeing as it is on an incline. As for the phantom truck, it is well known that the locals *hate* thrill-seekers and ghost-hunters visiting an otherwise peaceful countryside, sometimes to the point of chasing the interlopers back to other towns from whence they came. On the way to the cemetery is a message spray-painted onto the pavement, to be read like the opening to a Star Wars film: "NO GHOSTS. NO SANTA. GROW UP. GO HOME." Experienced ghost hunters have little luck gathering evidence, and attribute the stories to mere urban legend.

So, is this place even haunted? As the saying goes, truth is stranger than fiction ... and in this case, much more terrifying.

It was Halloween of 2004. I was sixteen years old, and my trick-or-treating years were behind me. There were four of us: Todd, Kris, Greg, and me. With Iron Maiden's "Fear of the Dark" blaring from the speakers, we embarked on a quest to find this unhallowed road. We missed our first turn because none of the signs bear the name of the road. Instead, they are cryptically labeled with initials to deter vandals from stealing signs with the ominous name spelled out in full. Our first destination was the bridge, which was underwhelming, to say the least. We continued west to the haunted woods and concluded that the ghostly lights of legend actually came from the car factory off in the distance, obscured by the trees. We turned around and headed for the cemetery. We figured if any ghosts were roaming the area, the cemetery would be our best bet.

We pulled off to the side of the road and approached the locked gate. For the first time that night, we felt uneasy, as if the fence wasn't the only barrier keeping us out. A single light post barely illuminated the black void surrounding it, its dreary orange light emitting a shrill hum. Todd was trembling, and considered staying in the car. Kris, who had been sarcastically taunting the ghosts all night, changed his tone as soon as we arrived. Greg and I were as stoic as ever but concurred that there was an undeniable sense of dread emanating from this place, and we were most certainly not welcome. So, we did the reasonable thing and went home! The end!

Just kidding. We totally hopped the fence.

Before I continue, I want to make it very clear that what we did was wrong. Although we were not using drugs or alcohol, vandalizing, or committing any other sort of destructive delinquency, trespassing is not only disrespectful, but also very dangerous, and I do not condone it. We were a bunch of teenage knuckleheads who knew better but did not give a fuck. If any readers are considering visiting this place or any location not open to the public, consider this a cautionary tale. Now, on to the story!

The cemetery was smaller than I initially imagined, and in complete disarray. The chain link fence was sliced open and pulled back. Gravestones were knocked over, spray-painted, some perhaps even stolen. The monuments that were still standing, though, were fascinating, to say the least. Some of them were towering obelisks or pillars. One was shaped like a giant open book on an altar, listing all the family members buried in the plot beneath. Another was shaped like the trunk of a tree; a very unsettling sight, especially in the middle of the night. The older graves were on the west end. Most of the markers were illegible, and a couple had an odd dip in the soil in front of them: a clear sign of a casket that had, over the years, caved in. We explored, peacefully and quietly, until we came across what seemed to be a tool shed. It was slightly tucked away from the property, surrounded by trees and vines, and just out of sight from the light. Kris took one look, and exclaimed, "NOPE!" before walking away to sit under a tree. Todd followed him. Greg and I shrugged and headed inside with a cigarette lighter to guide us in the dark. I guess a flashlight from home would have made too much sense.

Beyond the sliding wooden door, which was barely hanging onto its rusting rail, was an empty room with cinder block walls and a dirt floor that was littered with dead flowers, broken wood planks, and beer cans. I think one of them was a Schlitz, to give you an idea on how long this place had been run down. I spotted a strange shape on the east wall. I assumed it was a water stain from a roof leak since it reached the ceiling. Strangely enough, it was vaguely shaped like an eight-foot-tall human with a skeletal head and a slender neck upon shoulders without arms, and seemingly draped with a long cloak.

"Dude. Do you see that?" I whispered to Greg.

"Yeah," he replied. "We gotta show Todd and Kris."

As soon as he made the suggestion, a brilliantly evil plan came to mind. Once the other guys made it in, I would shine the light on the wall, point at the shape, exclaim, "HOLY SHIT OH MY GOD WHAT THE FUCK!" and run out, stranding them in the dark. Greg nodded in agreement, and we exited, stumbling over a thorn bush.

"Guys, come over here, you gotta see this!" I whisper-yelled. Kris shook his head and didn't budge. Todd approached, asking, "What is it? Just tell me!" I didn't answer; I just led the way trying not to crack a smile. Gosh, what a jerk I was.

Stepping over the bush and squeezing through the door, we entered the shed. Todd grabbed my coat and clung to me like a baby opossum. Slowly dragging our feet through the dirt, we approached the wall. I took a deep breath, flicked my lighter, and ...

"DUH—" was all I could utter. I stared blankly at the wall as the wall blankly stared back. The shape was gone. Todd, with a crack in his voice, whimpered, "You see it too?" I turned to look at Todd. Todd was looking at the north wall. I turned to look at the north wall, and there it was. Only this time, it wasn't on the wall. It was standing about a foot away from it, looming over us. Even to this day, it is nearly impossible to describe; it was solid black, yet translucent at the same time, and completely impossible to focus on, as if it was weaving in and out of existence at a rate I couldn't fathom. My delayed response to Todd was "... yup." He squealed and scampered out, stranding me with a being I had only heard of at this point: a shadow man. Suffice it to say, the prank backfired.

Wanting to run away but not wanting to turn my back on the entity, I awkwardly sidestepped my way through the door like an Irish folk dancer, tripping over the bush I told myself not to trip over. At a glance, I saw Todd diving behind the tree where Greg and Kris were waiting. I sprinted after them. We huddled together. Todd and I struggled to catch our breath while Greg and Kris frantically inquired what happened. "Shush!" I said sternly. Our eyes shifted to each other while slow, heavy footsteps emerged from the shed and onto the thorn bush with a distinct crackle. We peeked around the tree and back at the shed, but it was engulfed in shadows. The thunderous footsteps approached slowly, but with long strides. We bolted straight for Kris's car and drove off before all the doors were even shut. I turned to look through the rear windshield. There, in the middle of the road, against the dim light of the lone lamppost, stood the shape from the shed, blacker than the night surrounding it.

The four of us went home with one hell of a story to tell. We told our friends, and our friends told their friends. Soon enough, traveling down this road became a dare among my peers. One classmate claimed to see a shadowy figure step out of a cornfield and onto the road, causing her to swerve out of the way, nearly spinning out. Her description of the figure matched my encounter unequivocally. Another classmate, who had absolutely no interest in the paranormal, was merely driving through the area one night. His car stalled and shut off after driving through what he described was a black cloud. The most troubling account came from an acquaintance who claimed to see a dark mass huddled in the ditch that then pounced and chased after his Jeep. Between two glances through his rear-view mirror, he said it went from running like a large dog to running like a tall man with the hind legs of a digiti-grade. I wasn't sure what to make of his claim since this sounded less like a ghost and more like a demon, which I was not sure I believed in at that time. Fact or fiction, the plethora of new stories surrounding this place excited me, yet perturbed me at the same time.

I returned periodically over the next few years. Most nights were uneventful. Other nights would feel weird but without incident. My thoughts on this haunting would fluctuate with every visit. Was it a ghost? Was it a demon? Was it even real? I became obsessed with finding answers. In April 2005, Greg and I returned with a voice recorder. Standing by the tree-shaped monument, I asked if anyone would like to speak. What we heard immediately afterward nearly caused us to soil our britches: "BAH-A-A-A-AH!" A member of the livestock from a nearby farm had alarmed us. Obvi-ously, this was not paranormal; just a funny occurrence I wanted to share. Like Tony said in EPP Episode 77, "Sometimes, it's just a goat."

In May 2007, I was joined by my sister Marilyn and a couple of her friends. We decided not to enter, and just to hang out by the gate and look around. While scanning the yard of towering monuments, one in particular caught my attention. It stood all the way in the back, roughly eight feet tall. It was dark and seemed to be shaped like a column with an urn sculpted on top of it. I couldn't keep my eyes off it. Not even the chatting and giggling from the group could break my gaze. Something about it felt otherworldly and strangely familiar. Like I had seen it before, but somewhere else. My mind briefly entertained the thought that it almost looked like the shape I saw in the shed. That's when it began to move. It briskly traveled along the back fence before losing its form and vanishing altogether. Stunned, I asked if anyone else had seen it, but everyone else had their attention elsewhere. Soon afterward, the smell of sulfur filled the air. We took that as our cue to leave.

The same figure appeared on an otherwise uneventful night in June. We were making a U-turn at the end of the road by the cemetery. As the car's headlights shone over a field, we spotted a tall, dark figure standing roughly one hundred yards out. To make sure it wasn't a tree or some other trick of the eyes, we turned the car back around to look for it. This time, the figure was nowhere to be seen. Years later, my brother-in-law recounted a similar experience he had on the same road. He had not heard my story at that time.

That following August, I returned with a couple of friends I will call Shawn and Nancy. Shawn brought a fancy digital camera in hopes of capturing an image of the apparition I had told him about. He snapped a few photos around the graveyard before plunging into the shed. He pointed the camera at the wall after asking the entity to show itself. As the camera flashed, a rumbling growl filled the room. My first thought was maybe it was an animal. Shawn's first thought was to get the hell out of there. Whether or not it was an animal, that should have been my first thought, too. Whatever it was, it was not a goat.

Once we settled in Nancy's car and took off, I asked Shawn to show me the picture he just took. Taking his eyes off the camera's LCD screen, he looked at me with bulging eyes and slowly turned the camera around. What I saw still baffles me to this day. Sure enough, the camera picked up a tall, amorphous figure standing before us. Only it was white and wispy instead of dark and tenebrous. Talk about an unexplainable phenomenon about an unexplainable phenomenon! We spent the drive home discussing our evidence. Could what appears as a shadow person to the naked eye possibly appear lighter on camera? Was the flash a factor? Did the camera merely detect anomalous infrared light, as digital cameras are known to do? Was this an illusion like that damn dress (you know, the one that was blue-and-black or white-and-gold)? Sadly, the photo did not survive. Upon transferring the images to his hard drive, his computer deemed the memory card corrupted, and its contents were lost forever.

In July 2008, the road came up in a conversation between Bud, Lou, my other sister Olivia, her boyfriend Ricky, and me. Ricky, who was new to the group, and the area for that matter, had never been there. After hyping up the legend and sharing our experiences, we piled into Lou's Explorer and went for a drive. I made sure to grab a disposable camera on the way out. I wanted to capture this bastard on film if I couldn't do it digitally. Once we reached the cemetery, the same unwelcoming feeling overwhelmed us. Ricky and Olivia had no interest in entering the shed. While Bud and Lou jeered at them, I gave them a reassuring nod, as if to say they didn't have to if they didn't want to. Too bad I didn't follow my own advice. Bud, Lou, and I lined up to enter the tool shed. Bud pulled the door open as I snapped a photo. Lou jumped, screaming "Fuck that!" and ran back to Olivia and Ricky to tell them he saw something dark in the doorway. Undaunted, I stepped inside.

You know the feeling you get when you touch the screen of an old cathode ray tube television set? That prickly sensation of static electricity? Imagine that, combined with the sense of walking through spider webs. And I don't mean simply walking into spider webs, I mean *through* them, with every strand brushing and clinging against your very core instead of your skin. That's the best way I can describe what I felt as I passed the threshold. Unnerved, I turned around expecting to see Bud following behind me. I saw nothing. Apparently, he panicked and joined the others without mention. Abandoned once again, I felt a dark presence filling the room. My heart was pounding, and I gasped for air as chills ran down my neck. My legs began to quiver, and my eyesight became fuzzy. I wasn't sure if I was going to pass out or throw up. Terrified beyond the capacity of rational thought, I shambled out of the shed and made a beeline for the truck, wasting no time to join the others. I felt utterly drained, and I yearned for the safety and comfort of home. But the terror was far from over.

That night, I had a peculiar dream. I was walking through a forest on a lovely summer day, and I found myself entering a clearing. Throughout the glade were picnic tables, seated by various friends and family members. In retrospect, I realized what they all had in common: each of them had been to the road with me. They were all lively, chatting and laughing amongst themselves. Overjoyed, I began to approach this unexpected jamboree. Suddenly, time froze still. Red clouds swallowed the blue sky. The leaves of the trees withered, and the grass curled and turned gray. One by one, every person began to burn like a cigarette, and their ashes floated toward the sky, like snowflakes going backward in time. I stood aghast in horror, watching this hellish world evolve around me. In the center of the clearing, coils of black smoke slithered out of the ground, and materialized into the dark figure I had become all too familiar with. Without eyes, he glared at me. Without a voice, he spoke to me. Through sheer thought, he proclaimed himself a force not to be fucked with. By this point, I was well aware that this was a dream, but I knew that turning my back and running away would not bode well. So, I stood my ground, trying to force myself to wake up. With a howl that sounded like an avalanche, he lunged toward me. What felt like a jolt of electricity ran through every nerve within me, and I awoke to the absolute worst case of sleep paralysis I have ever had.

The worst part about it wasn't the inability to move, the inability to scream, or even the excruciating pain I felt as I struggled to regain control. No, it was the dark figure towering over my helpless body. His head crept closer and closer toward my face, and I was completely helpless to look away. He came so close that the darkness that embodied him engulfed my vision, and a grotesque face emerged. It was a putrefied human skull with the snarling muzzle of a bulldog. Its skin was shriveled and blackened with decay, oozing with blood and pulsating with maggots crawling underneath. The maggots dropped out of its empty eye sockets and gaping mouth and crawled all over my helpless body. The entire time this was happening, he was laughing an inhuman cackle that sounded like falling boulders. This went on long enough for me to contemplate that perhaps I had died and that this was hell. Another thought that was not my own thundered within my head: "*Never. Come. Back*." The face disappeared, and I could finally see my bedroom from the glow of a red, digital alarm clock. The time was 3:33 a.m.

As terrified as I was when I came to, I shrugged it off as merely a dream. I've had sleep paralysis in the past. Five times in my life thus far, including that occasion. I never attributed it to anything paranormal, despite how unsettling such an experience can be. I've also taken supernatural happenings during sleeping hours with a grain of salt. A mind is a mysterious machine, especially when it comes to dreams.

Alas, no amount of skepticism could have prepared me for what Olivia told me later that day. She, too, had dreamt that she was attacked by a tall dark figure, just like the one I had described to her for all of these years. She didn't have sleep paralysis, but she remembers waking up around 3:00 a.m. that night. I called Bud to ask if he had a nightmare as well, but he didn't. In fact, he didn't sleep at all that night. He said he was too busy hiding from a shadowy figure lurking outside of his window until 3:00 a.m. or so. It became apparent to us that this entity followed us home that night, and tormented us for disturbing the sacred resting place. As a repeated offender of kicking the spiritual wasps nest, so to speak, my punishment was more severe. Forever shaken by that nightmare, I vowed never to return after that night. As for the disposable camera, all the photos failed to develop.

For most people, this would be the end of the story ... but I am not most people. Don't try this at home, kids! I began seeking answers in demonology.

Though I was well versed in the paranormal before this time, I had always thought demonology was too outdated and dogmatic for something so beyond our understanding. I assumed most of our knowledge on demons was the product of primeval zealots and Hollywood. It took some suspension of disbelief on my part to even consider researching such arcane lore.

In my studies, I came across the name of a particular demon that resonated with me. I will not dare share its name, but I will say it is in fact featured in the Lesser Key of Solomon, and strangely enough, it phonetically coincides with the county that the road is located in. A Grand Duke of Hell with the heads of a man, a dog, and a griffin, commanding thirty legions at his disposal, his specialty is—get this—the marshalship of hauntings in tombs and cemeteries. Abashed, I felt like my personal ghost story was turning into a Dungeons & Dragons campaign.

I consulted with some friends who were also occult enthusiasts. Their interpretation was that this was a minion of the demon, a member of the thirty legions to carry its bidding. This makes sense because, well, there are quite a lot of cemeteries in the world. The three heads represent the forms these spirits can choose to manifest into. Since this was a township cemetery that was never affiliated with a church, it may have been vulnerable to a demonic infestation. Such beings are said to inhabit cemeteries prone to desecration. With the onslaught of interlopers seeking scares throughout the years, the entity could thrive and sustain itself by feeding on their fear. This makes me wonder what else could be lurking in the midst of other famous legends and paranormal hot spots across the globe.

True to my word, I have never been back at that cemetery. From what I understand, the tool shed has since been demolished, a local paranormal group has undertaken a restoration project, and police are on constant patrol in the area. For years, I haven't heard any new ghost stories from the road until just recently. A friend of a friend claims to have lost a cellphone in the cemetery. Upon calling her lost phone in an attempt to locate it, she received a "Hello?" from her own voice on the other line. Since this is not my story, I cannot claim it to be true, nor do I wish to inquire any further. The combined vigilance of the locals, the police, and the dark entity no longer make it worth investigating. Was I foolish for perpetually seeking answers in my youth? *Oh, definitely.* But these experiences have equipped me with the mental tools and knowledge that have served me well during some of my other experiences, which I will be sharing with you very, very soon. Until then, thank you, Tony and Jenny, for the show, and thank you, fellow listeners, for sharing your stories as well.

# DISAPPEARING CEMETERY HOUSE

The concept of a once-human ghost, or even that of an angel or demon, seems to be much easier to understand and accept as a facet of the supernatural than the ghost of an inanimate object or building. Over the course of doing this show, we have heard several stories of buildings appearing and disappearing in front of the same people in the same day—buildings that appear to be as real as the one you may be in right now. Why would buildings be ghosts, though, if they are not, and have never been, conscious beings? It makes us question the requirements for something of the past to return.

We once heard a story from a hiker about a cabin in the woods that went from being fully operational at the start of her walk, with its lights on and residents living in it, to becoming an abandoned, burned out hulk when she returned past it in the same hour. Why would a building present itself in two different ways, or better yet, how is it doing this?

In this story, we hear about a ghost house located near a graveyard that local legend says will appear and disappear, depending on the day and who is around at the time. Why and how a ghost building is able to do this baffles us more than most of the stories we share that involve beings who once walked—or did not walk—the earth. Linda shares her experience:

> I've been an EPP at ghostpodcast.com for a year now, and am going on my second year this week. I absolutely love your show. I have my daughter, Natalie, to thank for that. She's the one who told me about your podcast, and I'm so glad she did. I just surprised her with an EPP gift subscription, and she can catch up on all the episodes.
>
> My daughter was listening to one of the very early EPP episodes, perhaps one of the first ten, when she heard you speak of a disappearing house and an infamous cemetery. I can certainly fill you in on both. This cemetery is located in a suburb of Chicago. The graves

here date back to the mid-1800s. Sadly, many of these graves have been desecrated by the populace who frequent the cemetery. The sheriff's police patrol the area inside and out once dusk has fallen, as the cemetery is closed to everyone at dusk. Supposedly, law enforcement has found signs of devil worship going on, along with wire strung between two trees! The obvious reason for this wire is to hurt someone or worse yet, decapitate anyone who has been scared shitless by one of the pranksters and is running away. I'm assuming this occurs at night when somehow these evil people sneak in without being seen by the police. I know if they are caught in there after dusk, they will be arrested.

This cemetery was featured on a ghost TV series, which was pretty true to fact. There was a photo taken by a young lady in the graveyard of a ghostly woman dubbed "the Madonna" sitting on a gravestone looking toward the ground. This picture was taken with infrared film back in 1991, I believe, with an automatic advance 35mm camera. There was no way for her to doctor the film, and she has the original negative. The picture and negative were verified as genuine by a well-known photo expert. I believe you can google this and see the actual photo. It's amazing.

I've been to this cemetery quite a few times with a friend of mine who, like me, loves anything paranormal. While we were there, her ghost meter went off three separate times. It was just her and me in there at the time. Was this a spirit? We didn't know. Maybe the spirits were upset at the vandalism and criminal activity that has been going on at their final resting place and they're restless. We didn't see any wire between the trees, but we also didn't venture off the path too much because the brush is very thick. Perhaps the activity happens off the path, and if you're just looking for a haunted place to walk and you're not aware of the dangers beyond all the trees and bushes, you may encounter these jerks. Any normal person would not expect to be running out of the woods and right into a wire!

As for the disappearing house, I have seen it, although it was not actually in the cemetery. Back in maybe 1973, I was with my boyfriend and another couple when we decided to find this haunted graveyard. I had an idea of where it was, but I'd never been there. We drove for a few minutes and turned down a road we thought was the way into the area. The weird thing about this road was that it was so narrow, like a bridal path for horses. There were tall trees on each side of this narrow road, and it was very desolate. The sun had just about gone down at this time.

We were about to start backing up the car to get back on the main road when this house appeared to the left, as if out of nowhere. We all saw it and thought it was a strange place for a house, being hidden in all the huge trees and on such tiny road. It was a Victorian-type farmhouse with two stories and a wrap-around front porch. There were amber glows from lamps in the windows, which had sheer shades or sheer curtains on them. It was beautiful. We all sat there for a moment staring at this house that had just suddenly appeared. I'm sure we would have seen it as we were coming up that little road, but it wasn't there until the last second. We backed out onto the main road and eventually found the cemetery.

I truly don't think we walked inside the graveyard at this time because it was getting dark and we knew there were probably other people in there that would scare the hell out of us. I don't know if any of the awful stuff was going on in there back then, but I knew a lot of teenagers hung out in there.

Apparently, earlier in our journey, we had made a wrong turn. When we were on that narrow road with the big house, we'd been a little less than a half-mile from the cemetery. We must have been intrigued so much by that house that we wanted to see it again on the way home, so we drove down the road that we thought we had been on earlier when we were looking for the cemetery. We drove up and down this path, looking for that narrow little road that would lead us to the house. We found nothing. Not only did the house disappear, but so did the road that would get us there. I can remember this event like it happened last week. It is such a vivid memory.

The stories I've heard about this mysterious house say that it had been seen inside the actual cemetery. I can honestly say, even back then, there would have been no place in that cemetery where a house would fit in. Maybe because of the proximity to the cemetery, people believe that the house is inside the burial grounds, when in reality, it's about a half-mile northwest of it. But that road is gone, along with the house! I hope you enjoyed my story. I have several more that I'll write in. I love your show.

# NO CHECKOUT TIME

The start of a new relationship can be a fascinating time. It's a time of many firsts, some of which can be uncharacteristic of the people living them out. At times, these firsts can take a couple to unknown and sometimes haunting locations, like the ones we hear about in this story.

In what should have been an exciting and bizarrely romantic adventure through a once grand but now dilapidated hotel, a couple wound up finding more than just broken windows and peeling plaster. One of them felt and experienced the presence of former guests who'd never checked out. What message did this dead guest have for the date, and why were they making themselves known to only one of the date participants? And did this experience help or hinder the relationship? Andrew shares this haunting experience from his younger days:

At the time of this story, I was a photojournalist in Dallas/Fort Worth at one of the TV stations. One of my favorite things to do was to shoot video essays of old buildings. I have always been drawn to classical architecture. In North Texas, there is not a lot of it. While covering news stories out that way, I was always fascinated by a hotel that was something of a white elephant in a nearby small Texas town. It was fourteen stories tall with hundreds of rooms, a massive tower, and spooky but beautiful Spanish Colonial architecture. The hotel was opened in the first part of the 20th century to take advantage the natural health craze. During that part of the century, the area's natural mineral water, with its small amount of lithium, drew people from around the world, with many guests staying for months at a time. All of the A-list movie stars from the 1930s through the 1960s stayed at this hotel. Bonnie and Clyde were said to have had their last steak dinner at this hotel before leaving for their final shootout in Louisiana. Like many old abandoned buildings, this one had many tales surrounding it, some true, some not. This hotel closed for good in the early 1970s.

After contacting the property manager and asking for permission to do the video essay, I went out and was not disappointed. I interviewed some people that had worked there in its heyday. The video turned out great. My goal had been to record the history and architecture, not to do a ghost story. The ghost story happened a couple of years later.

It does seem some old buildings lure people to them. This hotel drew me in. I became good friends with the building manager and the locals that gave tours on the weekends. Before I knew it, I was doing tours every Saturday. This lasted for two-and-half years. It was a blast taking people around the hotel. Many locals on the tours had their own stories about the hotel in its prime. Most had never been inside; it catered to the elite.

During the holiday season and my final few months at the hotel, it was decided that the maintenance man and I would hang Christmas lights on the exterior of the building, from top to bottom. It was quite an undertaking for two people, but we did it. I ended on up on floors I had never been to before, securing lights to the window frames. It was creepy, but nothing strange happened. I'm sure I muttered a few times into thin air that I was "just working. I would be gone soon." The lights went up without a hitch, and the hotel looked amazing. For the first time in thirty years, this amazing hotel was lit for Christmas!

Up to that point, I had not been at the hotel at night. It was different at night, to be sure. At that time, the grand lobby was still in decent shape. With the darkness and the chandeliers lit, all the dust and water damage faded away. You had the feeling, at any moment, a bell captain would tap you on the shoulder and politely offer to take your bags.

I was proud of the Christmas lights and wanted to show them off to a girlfriend I had only been dating for a couple of weeks. I didn't know her that well, but I found out much more about her after a trip to the hotel. So on a cold December night, Emily and I arrived at the hotel. I'll confess that I was nervous about being in the hotel at night, but "as the man," I put those fears aside. As long as I had a flashlight, I told myself, I would be okay.

Note that I have been from the top to bottom of the hotel, and I never saw or heard a thing. If I did, I would not have come back. There were times I felt like there were spirits around, but they seemed to like me. They knew I was only there to help. I can say there were times, on some of the floors not used for the tours, that I felt like I was almost walking through a crowd. But nothing ever tried to show itself or scare me. It would have been quite easy. It's impossible to get out of the hotel quickly from the upper floors. The only exits are an old hand-crank elevator and the dangerous, cramped fire stairs.

The hotel looked amazing as we got into town. You could see the lights from miles away. I was excited to show her the place; it was going to be a good night. My fellow tour guides had turned on the lobby lights for me earlier in the evening to make it easier to navigate. The breaker boxes were in a room off the lobby that I did not like. I couldn't tell you why; it just felt wrong. But there we were, in the lobby at night, with the whole place to ourselves.

I showed Emily around the hall; it's quite beautiful, with massive Spanish iron chandeliers and eerie, Gothic plaster faces looking down from the pillars. She seemed interested, if not a little distracted. I could understand, but was I staying strong. I figured if I got nervous, she would freak out.

After the lobby tour had been completed, I ushered her to the original hand-crank elevators, art deco doors and all, and headed to the top floor for a tour of the

Cloud Room, with its windows that overlooked the city, and then on to the tower. We stepped in. I moved to my left to operate the crank. As I looked up, I noticed that she was wedged in the corner diagonal to me, as far away as she could get. I thought this was strange. She was a good six feet from me. She looked uncomfortable, but I carried on. I have a tendency to overlook the obvious. I left the doors open so I could see which floors we were passing; each is marked on the concrete wall as you go by.

Floor after floor speed by. I slowed to the top floor. Emily stayed in the corner and said nothing. All the levels were marked with numbers in white paint, but oddly, the top floor said Cloud Room in red. Trying to be funny, I said "redrum." I found out later she heard "murder." Emily had never seen *The Shining*. She must have thought I was nuts. So, there she was, fourteen floors up in a dark, abandoned hotel with someone saying "murder." Fun.

We got out of the elevator, and I showed her around the Cloud Room. She stuck very close to me. I could tell at that point she was freaked out, but I was determined to show her the tower, which is accessed from that floor. I didn't know at the time that getting back in the elevator was the best thing to do. She knew. I would find that out later. After a short look around the Cloud Room, we headed behind the elevators to a dark hallway that led to the tower access. I thought the tower would be romantic.

Remember what I said about missing the obvious?

The air was tense at this point, but nothing had happened that would turn me back. Honestly, if I thought something was up, I would have been out of there. I just thought she was nervous about being in this spooky building, but a man carries on, right? With a flashlight lighting the way, we made the turn for the hallway to the tower. She was behind me. About halfway down the hallway, she literally jumped on my back, damn near knocking me over. She scared the shit out of me. I asked her what was wrong; she only said that she heard something behind us. Being only steps away from the stairs to the tower, I carried on.

The poor girl. But I wanted to get to the top and show her the 35-foot windows that overlook the city, and I must admit, I wanted to see them at night, too.

The tower is super creepy even during the day, so you can only imagine what it's like at night. The lower portion of the tower houses the old-fashioned, original motors and electronics for the elevator and a spooky water tank, the perfect setting for a mad scientist's laboratory. In the middle, a spiral metal staircase leads up the top of the tower.

Well, we didn't quite make it all the way up. Emily stopped about halfway, only steps away from our destination. I could tell she was ready to get the fuck out. There was nothing romantic about any of this. I didn't press on moving forward; we made our way back the elevator. Again, she pushed herself diagonally away from me into the corner of the elevator. It seemed even stranger this time, since she was stuck to me the entire time we'd been on the top floor and in the tower. We made it back to the lobby no problem. It was a relief to be away from the darkness of the upper floor and have an exit in sight.

Back in the light of the lobby, I could tell she was ready to get out of there. Both of us laughed a little uncomfortably. She wanted to step outside. We sat on the steps, both relieved to be in the fresh air. I ask her if she was okay. What she told me she saw and heard was disturbing.

When we first went into the elevator, she saw three people standing in the middle: two women and a man dressed in clothes from the '30s or '40s. They were as real as you or me. That's why she was pressed into a corner. She told me they were caretakers of the hotel and that they knew me and were curious about why I was at the hotel so late at night. She said they were not there to be harmful, but from her perspective, they must have been frightening. With all this said, we can assume that this girl was seriously empathic.

Like I said earlier, I didn't know her that well. I couldn't believe what I was hearing. But it fit with what I saw in her actions.

She told me that when we were in the hallway to the tower and she jumped on my back, she had heard a sound like feet dragging along the concrete floor, like someone was floating in the air with the toes of their shoes just touching the floor. Creepy, right? She said that the caretakers had followed us the entire time, back onto the elevator and to the lobby. As we sat outside in the cold air with the lobby in sight through the tall, wood-paned windows, I asked her if they were still there. She looked over her shoulder and said they were gone. I've got to tell, you my hair was standing up all the way back to the city.

We stopped dating soon after our little tour of the hotel. I don't think the ghosts had anything to do with it. It was probably the "redrum" comment. But you never know ...

# GHOSTLY BREWS IN SAVANNAH

Do alcohol and ghosts mix? Some people will claim that alcohol opens them up to the supernatural world; others will say it shuts them off. We've even had stories of people claiming to fall into and out of possession after drinking too much. Is this a bad excuse for being drunk? That is often up to the observer to decide. It is important to note, however, that we have heard some very convincing cases of inebriated people suddenly knowing languages and possessing knowledge that the sober version of the individual would not know. It makes you stop to ponder the question at hand.

In this story, we don't hear about the mixing of alcohol and passion. Rather, we hear about the ghost of a little girl who wanders the halls of an old pub and makes herself known to select patrons. Does she have a message to deliver? Will she have a story to tell the innocent customers who simply sought out a pint?

Our listener Mea shares this story from Savannah, Georgia, one of the most haunted cities in America.

Today, I had a coworker ask me what my worst experience was working in the tour industry in Savannah. I'm always hesitant to talk about it since some people feel this stuff doesn't exist, which is funny, because it used to be part of my job! One of my least favorite spots, if not number one, is the brewery in town. The brewery was built in the 1800s and was once a hotel. It held many lives: a man died in a duel, a woman was supposedly shoved downstairs to her death, and a lion was housed there, among many other events.

One fun pastime is hopping onto your buddies' tours from time to time. Pub-crawls usually end in the brewery. I used to joke that it was because they wanted you drunk enough to handle going upstairs. The lower floor of the brewery is open to the public, and is known for its beer. The upper, unrenovated floors are widely known and have been witnessed by many to be seriously haunted. The brewery has attempted to renovate and serve on that level but simply couldn't, due to workers leaving the job, and most famously, for glasses flying off tables and breaking constantly. However, some tour companies have access to this floor during their tours. I absolutely hate this place, and have countless stories of my friends and their customers being hit, pushed, bruised, and often choked.

Especially if you are sensitive, you grow accustomed to constantly being "on" in Savannah—there's a lot of weird, old feelings around. I'll try to stick to what

I've experienced firsthand. The first time I ate at the brewery, I was unaware of its past. I was mostly excited to try the beer sampler as a college kid, and was seated toward the billiards room. I distinctly remember how sickening it felt: the hair on my arms stood up, and I did not like having my back facing the wall. I felt as if someone was behind me. I felt someone brush up against me distinctly, but tried to tell myself it was just a draft. I kind of blew it off and left a couple hours later, feeling much better after a few beers.

When I had my first encounter there, I had stopped by for lunch with friends. I went to use the bathroom at some point. The door was heavy and loud, and my friend Morgan stepped in too. Midway through, I realize I don't have any toilet paper, and seeing Morgan's shoes and shadow waiting, I ask her to pass me some. She didn't respond, so I said it again. I end up having to do the awkward waddle out the stall (TMI, I know), only to find that no one was there. I finished my business and got out, feeling unsettled. Only then did it occur to me what the shoes looked like: T-strap heels, a very '20s-era shoe, as if they were leaning against the wall. Disregarding this, I got back to the table and laughingly told Morgan that I had been talking to her but she wasn't there. Everyone said, "She's been here the whole time." I must've looked pretty sickly at that point—Morgan noticed—especially as I realized that I would have heard a person leave, given that the door was so loud. I never went to the bathroom there again without a friend in tow, and even when I did, I felt extremely uncomfortable.

My second experience was at the end of one of those pub-crawls I mentioned.

My boyfriend and I went, and I reluctantly trudged up those creaky stairs to the unfinished floor. While my friend, a guide, told her story, I saw a little girl wander into a hallway on our right. Knowing it would be extremely unlikely for a kid to be on our tour, and not wanting to look crazy or obvious, I casually walked over and peered down the hallway. The floor was only beams. As I mentioned, this place is very unfinished, and it will remain that way if the stories are true; whatever's there does not want it completed. The little girl casually balanced on them, and I immediately knew she was not real, and not what she appeared. Something was very unnatural about the way she balanced on them. The laws of physics didn't really apply to her, and there was something too innocent about her gait. I felt extremely nauseous, but I knew she wanted someone to follow her. I calmly made my way to the front of the line to get the hell downstairs, and was grateful it was nearly over.

One of the scariest occurrences was something I didn't witness but saw in photographs. One thing you don't think of prior to working in the tour industry is that you end up in everyone's vacation photos. Many people want to snap a picture of you or with you, and like a good hospitality worker, you always oblige. Another professional hazard is that you hang out with many mediums, psychics, and tend to take home ghosts. A guide I worked with began noticing that digital pictures of her weren't coming out, meaning they were consistently distorted in some way. Soon, she saw they were distorted in a very particular way: there was always an orange aura, or glow, around her. Over time, we saw several developed photos of these tours, and there was consistently, very clearly, a large orange outline of a man. This man had to have been 6'4" and was always directly behind her. These photos were taken during different tours, usually outside on the front steps of the brewery. Around that time, a psychic who had no knowledge of the photos warned her that a malevolent entity was very much interested in her. I felt very frightened for her.

Needless to say, that is not a place where I choose to hang out often. I would say that place is less about particular entities, and more about an overall, disorienting, angry feeling. Many sensitives believe a portal exists there, which I'm certainly no expert on. I've learned a lot since that time, and one of the things I've learned is that some places are too damn much. Love y'all, and take care.

# CHAPTER 6
# SPIRITS FROM THE PAST

They say, "The past is never far …" But in some ghost stories, the past never seems to have ended. In some of the more unique haunted stories we've heard, the past seems to be able to interact with the present on a very real and dangerous level. The idea of an echo of a ghost soldier marching through a forgotten battlefield is far from the only way history seems to catch up to the present on its own terms.

## GHOSTS ON A TRAIN

Can residual energies interact consciously with the present? That is the question this story begs us to ask. A young man gets on a train with one goal in mind: to get home safely. What he encounters on that train appears to be the echoes of war from many years ago. What is shocking about this story is that these echoes of history appear to see and hear this traveler in present day, some going as far as to protect him from the atrocities of the battle that is occurring before their very eyes.

What is going through the mind of the ghost soldiers attempting to protect the civilian who is not from their time? Is the modern-day man appearing as a ghost to the soldiers in a different place and time?

So many questions are left after hearing this account. It's truly one of the most haunting and intriguing stories we've heard on our program. Brad shares his experience:

> When I was young, I was in the Army and stationed in Heilbronn, Germany, during the '80s. In the spring of 1984, I had a weekend off, so I spent the day sight-seeing the local area between Heilbronn and Stuttgart with friends. This was followed by an evening of beer drinking with buddies in downtown Stuttgart. We drank and played pool, foosball, and darts; it was a very good time. At some point, I let everyone know I was headed back to Heilbronn early, as I was running low on money and still needed to get back to the barracks. I was heckled a little, and some offered me money for beers, but I refused and left it at that, and said I'd see them in the morning.
>
> It was late, after 10 p.m. I took a taxi to the train station and got a ticket to Heilbronn. It's a short train ride, about thirty-five to forty minutes. I was alone on the platform when I thought I heard children yelling, but I saw no one. I told myself that it must be my good buzz making me hear things. A few minutes later, when the train slowly screeched into the station, I thought I heard machine gun fire!

I hit the ground and started looking around, then
realized how foolish I must have looked, as there was
nothing there. I got up, brushed myself off, and entered
the train, looking around and hoping nobody saw my
actions. At this point, I was all alone, sitting in the
middle of the train car. The train jerked then started to
move. Some of the overhead lights flickered on and off
quickly then stopped. *This is kind of creepy,* I thought.

About fifteen minutes went by as I sat there yawning
and trying to stay awake, thinking *damn, this is boring,*
as I looked out the window. I noticed it was very dark
and black outside, more than usual. As soon as I made
this realization, I heard guns cocking. My head immediately snapped around to my one o'clock position where
I was startled to see five German soldiers, fifteen feet
away, facing me with machine guns drawn. The soldiers were partially transparent; I could kind of see the
seats through them. "What the fuck!" I blurted out as I
ducked to the floor, closing my eyes. I heard the *ratt-
tatt-tatt-tatt* of the machine guns. *How strange it is that
I don't hear the bullets striking anything.* I peeked up
over the seat and there was nobody there but a slight
puff of smoke, like cigarette smoke.

I sat back in my seat, agitated, scared, and confused,
all at the same time. I was hyperventilating a little,
when I felt a calming tap on my shoulder from behind.
I looked backward and upward to find two semitrans-
parent U.S. Army soldiers standing there. I remember
this vividly: The black soldier had green eyes. He was
holding an M1 Carbine, putting his finger to his lips

*shhhhhh*ing me, his teeth bloody; then he hand-signaled for me to get down.

The white solider was quite unshaven, smoking a cigarette, and holding an M1 Thompson Submachine Gun. I slid down to the floor and looked straight up. The two soldiers pointed over me and fired, *burrrrrpp, pop pop*. There was some yelling in English and German, and children screaming in terror. Then I heard the *ratt-tatt-tatt-tatt* of the German machine guns. The white soldier got hit in the upper chest several times. He thrashed in agony, blood spewing from his mouth. The black soldier looked at him, shouted, "NOOOOOOOOOOOO!" before he, too, was hit in the neck, blood squirting from the wound like from a drinking fountain.

I closed my eyes and started screaming, "Shit, shit, shit, this can't be happening, stop, stop, stop, please, stop!" It got quiet. I opened my eyes, picked myself up off the floor, and saw that everything had vanished, except for the cigarette smell in the air.

I sat down, literally shaken, scared, and confused, trying to rationalize what I just saw. Again, I was startled; I started to hear children laughing, making me jump big time. I looked out the window, and I saw the reflection of about ten typical boys and girls, I guess about thirteen years old, all of them staring at me laughing. They pointed in my direction, and their laughs turned to horrid screams as their bodies were riddled by bullets and their faces turned to decomposed globs of bone and flesh, scaring the shit out of me.

I yelled as the lights flashed on and off a couple of times. I heard the train screech, which caused me to blink a few times. The kids were now gone, just as the others had disappeared. I sat in my seat for the next few minutes, dazed and confused and scared, but okay. I snapped out of it as the train jerked to a stop in Heilbronn.

I have kept this story to myself for many years, leaving parts out, making light of it, and telling it differently all together, as I thought people would think I was drunk or hallucinating. I'm telling of this haunting, or should I say "ghost battle," in its entirety now, after doing some research decades later.

I discovered there was a battle for Heilbronn between the American and German armies toward the end of WWII. This nine-day campaign involved heavy, intense house-to-house, room-to-room fighting. Buildings, soldiers, women, and children were all caught in the crossfire. The weird thing is that the Americans snuck in across the Neckar River and along the railway system to surprise the German opposition. Even more unearthly, this battle involved a sizable number of Hitler youth. The death toll was around 2,000 Americans and Germans, with soldiers and civilian casualties. I like to think I was witnessing some side battle that occurred during the nine days of fighting.

Is it possible the energy can be left or transferred to an area or location due to some heinous event? Part of me says it could've been the Hitler youth playing with me, as at that time I was an American soldier, or was it the Americans letting me know about the heinous attack and killing of innocent children by the Germans? The only reason I lean toward the second of the two explanations is that the two American soldiers were acting like they were trying to protect me as if I were a child, telling me to stay down and keep quiet.

# BROTHER'S CABIN

The idea of a nearly expense-free vacation is an appealing one. Who wouldn't love to take some time away from the norm and get away for a weekend? However, is the getaway worth it when there is a ghost involved?

This is the very question one man had to answer for himself when he was presented with this opportunity.

In this account of the paranormal, we see the level to which one will tolerate a haunting. For some, just a few unexplained bumps in the night would make for a trip-ending moment. However, for others it takes much more than just some noises, or even disembodied apparitions, to make a vacation end.

This is the story of Matt and his stay at a sibling's cabin.

My wife and I regularly go to a lovely beach community located about twenty minutes outside of Charleston, South Carolina. And, as with everything in and around Charleston, it's haunted as shit.

When we go, we regularly stay at her brother's beach house. When her brother first bought the house, it was run down and out of date. Now it's some immaculate piece of modern, new age design. The story I'm about to tell takes place when it was in its original condition.

We arrived at the beach house in late August 2014. He had just purchased the house three months prior, so it was still in rough shape and looked like no renovations had been done after 1989. Walking into the beach house, I just got this creepy vibe from the place. I'd be lying if I said that I was ever "paranormally inclined," despite my love for the subject. However, I felt like I would see things out of the corner of my eye and then look and nothing would be there. We knew there were bats in the fireplace, though, so the noises we heard coming from there were quickly explained.

The first night we got there, we were all exhausted from the long drive from Nashville to Charleston. We called it a night pretty early. The wife and I stayed on the first floor; her parents went up to the second floor.

Around 2 a.m., I woke up to a loud *SMACK!* sound that emanated from the main living room area. It sounded like someone had decided to pick up a thick book, walk up the stairs to the second-floor landing, and then drop it to the hardwood floors in the living room. My wife and I both woke up, so I walked out to see what it was, turned on all the lights, and saw nothing. I searched all over the place for the source of the noise, because trust me, I'd rather have a logical explanation for it than think we were staying in a ghosted-up beach house, but there was absolutely no explanation.

While a lot of people might chalk that up to "well, maybe you heard it in a dream," how did my wife and then her father, who at breakfast the next morning confirmed he heard the same thing, get awakened by the same thing?

You may be a little underwhelmed by my story so far. I know. But wait, it gets better.

First, I have to tell you that I have a little bit of a problem. I love professional wrestling. Yes, I know it's fake and scripted. However, most of reality TV and every other source of media entertainment is scripted and fake. Anyway, it was a Monday night, which meant wrestling was on TV. My wife and her parents wanted to go out to dinner, and I couldn't miss my fight, so I just told them to go on, and I'd stay at the beach house and figure out dinner myself. So off they went, and I stayed and started watching my wrestling.

After about an hour, I decided to go to the kitchen and make myself a drink, which would have been my first of the evening. So, I got up from the couch and start walking toward the kitchen. The kitchen was con-nected to the living room and separated by an island. If you looked to your left from the island, your gaze went down a hallway that led to a bedroom. Well, while walking to the kitchen and approaching that island, something told me to look to my left, down that hallway and into the room. And to this day, I can't explain what I saw. Rather, I can explain it, but I can't really under-stand it. When I looked to the left, I saw a pair of legs walk from the room down the hallway.

That's it. Just legs. Nothing above the legs. I wish I could have seen more detail, but the legs walked by in a shuffling fashion and the outline was blurry and nondescript. I'd never in my life felt the cold rush I felt at that exact moment. It was as if somehow I had been transported to the middle of Antarctica wearing only my shorts. All the hairs on my arms were raised, like a cat sensing danger. I stood there, just looking at the doorway, ready for those torso-less legs to walk back in the other direction, but it never happened. I waited around a minute or two before I moved. I walked down the hallway and into the room and saw nothing. The edge had disappeared; no longer were the hairs raised, nor was I chilled. There was absolutely no sign of anything in that room.

I felt like an idiot. *Do I tell the wife and her parents and risk being called an idiot or getting accused of having one too many? Or should I just tell them the truth?* I told them the truth.

Everyone agreed that they'd feel weird if they were alone in the house, especially late at night or early in the morning. But no one experienced what I did.

A few nights after that, we went on a ghost tour in downtown Charleston, and I asked the guide what exactly it was that I had seen.

His explanation was this: there was an old saying explaining that if you just saw legs, then the ghost you had seen had died in a horrible way. He explained that some of the Civil War soldiers had been blown in half by cannonballs and maybe that's what I saw, since this whole area was just a cornucopia of Civil War–era history.

A few days passed and nothing out of the ordinary happened, at least nothing we had noticed. Then, another night came about where wrestling came on and the wife and her parents decided to go out to eat while I stayed home. From the living room area, you can look up from the couch to see the second-floor landing. From that view, you can see the two rooms up there and the bathroom. When I first sat down on the couch to watch wrestling, I had looked up at the second floor and noted to myself that all the lights were off, thinking that if they had left the lights on up there, I was just going to turn them off.

About an hour into wrestling, I looked up at the second-floor landing and saw that the bathroom lights had been turned on. Now just to be safe and to rule out ghostly shenanigans, I texted the wife to ask if her parents had left the lights on when they had left. She replied back with, "No, they turned off everything, you know Mom is meticulous about that stuff."

I just responded with "Oh." And I don't know how to explain it, but right when I texted her and she con-firmed the lights had been off, I looked up again, and the lights were off.

I have this thing where if I think a ghost is nearby, but I can't see it, I just talk aloud, so that's what I did here. I went, "Okay, cool, we have an understanding. You're here; I know you're here. Let's just be cool as shit with each other, and you do your ghostly thing, and I'll do my human thing, and I only ask that you don't try to scare my ass with anything, cool?" Of course, there was no response, but I felt better. I wasn't going upstairs to investigate.

Now, let's fast forward a few months. After the trip, we returned to Nashville. Everything went back to normal. We checked in with my wife's brother and his wife to inquire as to whether they had ever encountered anything weird or paranormal. That was met with a resounding "no!" which I kind of laughed off. *It's fine*, I thought. *I'm not worried about that.*

Around March of the following year, I was sitting downstairs in the living room at my place. My kids were with me, and we were watching *Billy Madison* on TV. We love the movie and tend to act out a lot of the scenes we like. So, because we're big movie nerds and even greater Adam Sandler movie geeks, we started acting out a scene. While we were all in the living room acting, the window and doors were open and you could see outside perfectly clearly. In the middle of our laughing and goofing off, we stopped dead in our tracks and looked at the door, where we saw a shadow of someone walking by, and we watched as that same figure walked by the window. I immediately rushed toward the door and threw it open. The kids followed, and we all craned our necks in the direction the person we saw was walking. There was nothing there.

At this point, we hadn't said a word to each other. Quickly, I asked, "What did you see?"

My son said, "Someone walked by and it looked like a soldier."

My daughter chimed in. "Yeah, I could definitely see the gun he was holding in his hand that was rested upon his shoulder, like a shotgun."

Chills ran down my spine because I saw the same thing. I saw the hat, like so many Civil War soldiers had worn during that period, and I saw the outline of the rifle from his lower hand up to his shoulder, where it rested.

I don't think the two instances were related, but it is weird that both times, I seem to have encountered Civil War–era ghosts.

A few months ago, my wife received a text from her brother's wife, regarding to the beach house spirit. They have a son who's all of four years old, almost five. According to her brother's wife, their son had been playing in the room where I saw the torso-less ghost, and when he came out, his mother had asked him who he was talking to. He had been in there for quite a bit and seemed to be talking and enjoying himself. He replied simply, "The ghost."

He had never been told my story, nor would I think a four-year-old would be so devious to play a joke like that, months after the fact.

Now, the house has been renovated completely and is modern and chic, and I haven't seen or noticed anything out of the ordinary since the first trip. As I type this, I'm sitting at a table that is located in the area where I saw that first torso-less ghost. And while there isn't exactly an ominous feeling anymore, even at the late hour when I'm writing this, sometimes I get cold chills up my spine and have this urge to look at the second-floor landing area, the one that overlooks the beach. I don't want to and fight the urge to do so, but I know I will, and I know I'll see nothing. It doesn't make the feeling go away that there is still something here.

The house may have lost something with the renovations, but it's still here. It's not harmful or out to hurt anyone; it's just here. I've always felt it and still do to this day.

Anyways, I appreciate your guys' podcast. I started listening years ago and got the wife hooked, and we are both EPP members and listen multiple times a week. I just needed to get it off my chest and let someone else, someone who is maybe like me—skeptical, but intrigued—know that there is something out there we cannot explain.

# CHAPTER 7
# COMMUNICATING BEYOND THE GRAVE

Can our loved ones come back to deliver messages from beyond the grave? Sometimes the term "loved ones" is used loosely when it comes to this topic, which can make these experiences even more confusing—someone genetically related to you may send a message from the other side, but you might not have felt much for that person than casual recognition.

Important messages in this form can add a new level to how you view relatives who have passed, sometimes casting them in a redeeming light. Either way, millions of people around the world receive visits from deceased relatives, who bear either messages of importance to life here or confirmation of their existence on the other side.

## OUIJA WARNING

One of the most common items that we discuss on our program is the Ouija board. We have actually lost count of the number of inquiries we've received regarding unexpected consequences from using this device. Sometimes the unintended consequence is somewhat small, like some unexplained knocking, or maybe an unidentified breeze moving through a house. Other effects are much deeper and darker than that—possession, torments, life-changing and -altering events, and messages coming through that the living should never know about. You just don't know what you'll get when using one of these boards. That is where the problem begins.

When a product is marketed as a toy along with Mousetrap and Candyland, it's understandable that youth would be intrigued by this device that offers such mythical abilities. It's also understandable that one would not take it seriously and view it as some type of parlor trick or illusion. Those who have experienced the unintended consequences that come about after using the board know all too well that its powers are far beyond tricks.

In this story, we hear how some young people navigated the world that was manipulated around them after using the Ouija board. Alan shares his story.

> I started listening to your podcast today and felt compelled to tell my experience. I grew up in an old house that was located in Michigan on a lake called Lake St. Clair. This house was once used for a hotel and blind pig (speakeasy) during the Prohibition era. Local lore says that prominent Detroit and Chicago gangs used this home to conduct business. As a family, we could

only assume these were just stories. We had been living in the house for quite some time before anything raised suspicion otherwise.

At first, we just heard relatively benign noises that one could disregard as "just hearing stuff." Sounds like taps, knocks, and creaks would come from all over the house. We had a bull terrier with a keen sense of his surroundings. He would, at times, bark at walls or just stare down the hallway, so we would have to physically move him to another room for him to stop growling at thin air. I never thought anything of it, and my mother was pretty good at ignoring the situation, in the same way that you don't announce the elephant in the room.

These encounters started to escalate when I was thirteen years old and received a Ouija board as a birthday gift. I didn't even open it until summer, and my birthday is in January. During these summer months, my next-door neighbor and I had nothing going on, and on one stormy day (I know it sounds cliché) we pulled out the never-before-opened Ouija board and started to play at my place. Nothing really happened for a while, but we were persistent. It's not like we "believed" in ghosts. For fun, we would play with one another: one of us would move the finder to freak the other out, and we both fully knew that we were doing so.

At one point, my neighbor took her hands off, and I kept playing while she watched. I asked, "Is there anybody here other than us?"

I shit you not, that finder started moving. I jumped back, and she didn't believe me because of all the joking previously. It took a small amount of convincing, but we both jumped back on and asked again, "Anybody here other than us?" It moved to "E.J."

As children, because that is what we were, we kept playing and asking all kinds of questions—simple ones, like "what's my middle name?" and "what's my grandma's name?" and it answered correctly. We pressured early about it showing itself, but no luck. She and I talked with E.J for a couple weeks at most. Sometimes he would respond and sometimes he wouldn't. Within these couple weeks, we came across another "friend" by the name of Emily. Emily was truly a sweet entity and helped us tremendously, but I'll have to get back to that later.

After a few weeks of speaking with him, E.J. starting asking for favors and said he'd reveal himself if we did them. E.J.'s favors consisted of weird stuff, like moving other neighbors' property or moving objects in my attic to certain areas. One day, he asked to throw a dead muskrat into the lake. We looked for this dead animal for a while, and we started to give up. We were standing toe to toe, deciding whether to abandon this task or not, and we looked down, and there was the muskrat. It was almost as if it materialized out of thin air but we followed orders and threw it in the lake. I must state that we did not harm a single animal—the muskrat was already dead.

We ran back to the house, jumped back on the board, and tried to speak with E.J. It didn't take long for the board to respond once we were back in my room.

We sat down, placed our hands on the finder, and it instantly wrote, "Thank you."

I asked, "Who is this?" and the response will never leave me.

It wrote, "Devil."

We both freaked out, said goodbye, and closed the box. The next morning, we went back to area where we conducted the muskrat sacrifice (this is all I can think of it as) and there were three headless chicken's bodies and $666 in a white bag. Well, being kids, we thought it was odd, but we still took the money.

A couple nights later, my neighbor and I once again tried to summon whatever we could get, but to our surprise, we came into contact with Emily at this point. We asked all the same questions as we had E.J., but she responded very differently; it was genuine. She spoke about being killed in a car accident years before, and we were very interested in this contact. When we mentioned our recent actions, she told us not to speak to E.J. and talked about him being an evil man.

Emily said to go to my shed and open the door. We ran out of my house to my back yard and opened the door. We were met with a floating green orb that slowly morphed into a little girl. We stared for what seemed like an hour, but was really about three minutes. My neighbor and I then slammed the door in disbelief and ran to her house, where I spent the night. We didn't sleep that night, just stayed up talking about what we saw. Even though we were freaked out, we agreed that we felt safe. However, I went home the next morning and packed up the board.

This is when I started sleepwalking, having terrible night terrors, and thinking horrible thoughts. In the beginning of my sleepwalking episodes, my mother recalled watching TV on the couch with me sound asleep upstairs, when I would suddenly appear laying on top of the couch, staring down wide-eyed; this wasn't a one-time instance. Other times, she would hear me knocking and talking to her through her bedroom door, but when she opened the door, I wasn't there. During these nights, I would dream horrible things, such as my family being killed. I would sweat clean through my sheets and wake up at 3 a.m. on the dot.

I would sleep with my TV on and sheets over my head due to seeing shadows out of the corner of my eye. I would hear footsteps in the attic and hallway. I would hear my dog scratching on the bottom of the door and open the door in excitement to have my dog, but he wasn't there. I would see my sheets move slightly up then drop, like the sheet wanted it to play. One morning I woke up after another rough night to discover what looked like "the hanging man" from a Tarot deck infused into the grain of the wood on the back of my bedroom door, like it was naturally in the grain but still fully recognizable as the figure.

At this point, I was at a loss. I felt like I was helpless and just lived with it. My family members would just deal with it as well. We learned not to acknowledge it, but sometimes it was hard. Day or night, we felt like we were about to be grabbed, pushed, or tackled, but nothing ever touched us. Once we learned not to care, it only got heavy late at night, or if it was a very stressful time in the house, full of yelling and fighting.

This went on for a few years, then one day at school, I overheard a story about a Ouija board and butted in with my story. The other kids at school told me to get rid of it. I had never put two and two together. *Why didn't I get rid of it?* As soon as I got home, I ran inside, duct taped that box, and threw it away. That night was the calmest night my family had experienced in a long time. It's like we opened the door and had an unwanted guest leave.

This is just the tip of the iceberg when it comes to what some others experienced in that house; I tried to put the story in a nutshell. There is one more thing, however. A good friend of mine has always been intrigued by my experience and spoke to a coworker about my house. Well, this coworker had family living in that house before me. The owner was his uncle, had the initials E.J., and it just so happened that he hung himself in that house. As for Emily, I still wish I could have given her a proper goodbye or sent her on her way to the other side somehow. Years later, with the help of the Internet, I found out that there had been a car accident in front my house where a particular girl named Emily died. We have since moved and the house has been demolished, but things still linger in the night on the property.

Ever since this experience, I have nothing but compassion for those who have been through such trauma. All I have to say is you're not crazy, and in time, I was able to come to terms with my experience.

# DEATH BY THE BOARD

The moment someone opens the box to a Ouija board, places a planchette on the top, and begins to ask questions, I sincerely hope they understand the possibilities of what they are in for.

It doesn't take long after listing to our program to understand the true ramifications of what may appear to be a simple game. Often, the beings on the other end of the board have a far greater knowledge of our presents, pasts, and futures than we can begin to contemplate.

Are the voices and conscious bodies of knowledge on the other side of the board good? Are they evil? These questions can only be answered once the interaction has begun. Sometimes they cannot be answered until many days, or even years, have passed.

One of the questions we've always had about the boards' responses was, "Is the board always right?" It seems that in this next story, the board got close enough. For one individual, it got far too close for comfort, especially when it began to discuss her own demise. Alexis shares the story of her interaction with a Ouija board.

In the late summer of 2016, one blazing hot August night, I was home alone after work. I had gone through my parents' attic earlier, where I'd found an old Ouija board that appeared to have been unused for quite some time, as it was dented and dusted. The board was missing a planchette, but as I had nothing to do, I figured I would improvise. I took the board to my bedroom and placed it on my bed. I was wearing a planchette-shaped stone around my neck, so I took it off the chain and placed it on the board.

I was aware of the many rules that accompanied the Ouija board, such as the belief that no player should use it alone, and that one should be wary of the planchette making figure eights. Knowing what I did, that there was no other player to communicate with me, I took extra precaution and put a silver coin by the board to ward off the evil spirits, and I said a prayer before I began. Starting the session, I turned off the lights, turned on my camera to see if I could record an electronic voice phenomena (EVP), and asked my first question.

"What is your name?" The board spelled out a name I will not repeat here, but know it is was the name of a documented demon.

Despite remembering that name in a vague story I heard a time ago, I continued. "Where are you from?"

"F-I-R-E" was the next thing this spirit spelled out. Before I knew it, I could feel the planchette under me shake, and all over the board, it began to form rapid figure eights. Knowing this was a sign of evil, and that

I had already broken the rule of never playing alone, I thought there was no choice but to continue.

What I asked next was a pure mistake. "What do you want from me?" The planchette suddenly stopped on F.

What happened next shocked me. The board spelled out profanities toward me too vile to name. Once I knew how much hot water I was in for pissing off a malicious spirit, I tried to move the planchette to "Goodbye"—except it wouldn't move. I froze and chills rode up my spine. The room grew colder and colder by the second. All of a sudden, the board spelled out "I-M H-E-R-E." You could only imagine how much terror I felt, knowing that I blindly invited a nasty spirit into my life.

I stood there frozen, and my instincts urged me to turn the light on. Once I did, I still felt no relief from this situation. Headed back to the board, I said: "Please, now that you are here, I mean no disrespect, but what will lay ahead of me?

"D-E-A-T-H, O-C-T-O-B-E-R"

Feeling too fearful to continue this conversation, I quickly moved the planchette to "Goodbye" and stopped recording. I knew what lay ahead of me could not be good, so that very night, under the full moon, I broke the board into seven pieces and doused it and my bedroom with holy water. I then proceeded to the backyard to bury the board in the soil. The weeks that followed that fateful night were calm.

Weeks turned into months, and not a single abnormality appeared. Even with so much time passing, I couldn't bring myself to watch the recording of the session. I still had it on my camera, and I did not want to get rid of it in case one day I would gain some courage.

On the night of October 28, 2016, I was lying in bed listening to the Beatles like any other night. I was slightly distracted when I heard the fire alarm go off in the kitchen. As I went to investigate, I noticed one of my burners was on full blast, even though nobody was home. The stove was flaring off heat, so I went to turn it off.

When I returned to my bedroom, a shadowy, foggy mist appeared, clouding my vision. The mist smelled vile, of rotting eggs, and the smell alone started to flare up my asthma. I had been diagnosed with severe asthma two years back, and my lungs began to fill with mucus. As this happened, I struggled to breathe. I knew I was the only one home, so I had to dial 911 somehow. As I exited to the hallway, I noticed that the smell and the mist continued out there, and my chances of being able to talk from my asthma attack were minimal. Eventually, trying to breathe became exhausting, and I felt as I was being strangled, my lungs stinging with pain.

I lay down on the floor and everything went black. I woke up, and the first thing I saw was a paramedic staring me right in the eyes, with a pitying expression on her face. I was utterly confused, as the last thing I remembered was being home upstairs in the hallway.

Before I could speak, I noticed the defibrillator attached to me, which sent me into a panic. After the paramedic had calmed me down, she told me that one of my roommates came home from work and found me on the ground, purple faced.

My roommate could find no signs of breathing or a pulse, so she rushed the paramedics over to the house, and they had to revive me. Luckily, the roommate walked in nearly a minute after I had fallen, and knowing about my asthma, she knew what to do. To this day, I recall the horrifying events that took place as baffling, malicious, and purely terrifying.

I do not honestly know if it was the evil spirit that caused my brief death experience, or why I could not remember anything when I had no breath or a pulse, but I feel that the spirit certainly had an influence on it. I knew I had to watch the tape of that fateful August night, whether I liked it or not. There could have been something I missed, some other hint about the accident.

When I worked up the courage to replay it, I could not see any abnormalities on camera, but could hear it. A distinct, malevolent voice was saying to me, "You will regret this. And for this, you will suffer." Indeed, I was taken aback by this entire experience. The key advice that can come out of this is never to touch a Ouija board; if you find one, you should break it and bury it.

Talking to the undead is not worth what may happen to you next. You could become the victim to many evil things, or worse, you can learn things you shouldn't have knowledge of. It's not worth the risk.

# THE CB RADIO

As a child of the '80s who remembers a world pre-Internet, the first time I (Tony) saw a CB Radio in action was an incredible moment. A device that allowed you to talk to mystery people, whose names and personalities changed depending on your location, was exciting. The CB represented a whole world of information and conversations that could be had with the simple pressing of a button. Who would be on the other end once your message was sent out? It was a mystery and an adventure.

I remember as a teenager attempting to create a CB Radio station with an old CB and a large antenna I had purchased from a friend. I rigged up a way to "key the mic," or keep my feed going without interruption, and began to broadcast Top 40 radio hits of the time and talk between the songs as if it were a real radio station. I was young, naive, and clueless to the proper etiquette one should use when broadcasting on a CB channel, and this idea backfired.

When my show finally ended, I had almost every CB enthusiast in my hometown riled up and searching the neighborhoods for the strong signal, trying to figure out where it was coming from. I knew this because looking out my front window, I found a bunch of station wagons sporting large antennas driving up and down my road saying, "I think he's around here ... damn ... I lost his signal!" This event ended my CB broadcasting days.

In this story, we hear the story of another child who was excited and intrigued by the voices he picked up on the CB radio, only to find out that a voice on the other end might not have belonged to the living. Joey shares this intriguing story.

I was born and grew up in California, where I still reside. I have had so many "supernatural" or "paranormal" experiences in the tenure of my life that these words are almost pretentious to me. And the notion of someone being a skeptic is as silly as someone not believing that a million dollars exists because they have never seen that much money. Most of these experiences I have kept close to me or secret, as not to be singled out or labeled "paranormal" myself. The experiences that I have shared with people, I disguise as "ghost stories" that most listeners love and beg me to tell again.

Much like you, since I was a child I have been completely fascinated with radio, broadcasting, and other forms of long-range communication with any others who might be listening. My first memory of this interest is from when I was very young and my dad gave me an old CB radio he had bought at a yard sale. I was completely enamored and devoted all of my attention to this device. I refocused my devotion from playing "Contra" or having "dirt-clod wars" to communicating with others over CB. I met and chatted with so many CB and HAM radio dorks that the number is unfathomable. Among all of these people, each of whom was fascinating, only one stands out in my memory.

He was my age, and I met him via CB only a little while after I'd delved into this endeavor. We liked all of the same things: Ninja Turtles, Star Wars, He-Man, *The Lost Boys* ... I could go on and on, but it would be far too extensive. Above all, we both loved ghost stories and "creepy-ass shit." He indeed came to be the brother I never had, as my other three brothers were a bit younger and I was relegated to raising them by myself because both of my parents worked full-time jobs to provide. We were poor, but rich in love and the very simple things in life.

My regular fulfillment came from chatting with this best friend of mine, who I had never formally met in person. I still remember preparing dinner for my brothers, then hurrying them to brush their teeth, bathe, and get to bed promptly so that I could bask in my radio-wave indulgence. I couldn't wait to talk to my first (and only) best friend, who was the only kid who could spin a yarn of ghost stories better than I could. During the our early sessions, I asked him his name, and he said, "You can call me T-1000, or T, for short," and that he was from Wisconsin. He told me that his dad Jim was a local late-night radio station DJ in that area. I was completely flattered every time he would say, "Hey, you *need* to call the station, and my dad will put you on the air."

T was truly my dearest friend. We would chat damn near every day, and we would conduct special broad-casts for each other on our birthdays and on holidays like Christmas, Thanksgiving, and especially Halloween. Over time, I've maintained many relationships and jobs here and there, but nothing compared to my connection with T and my love for radio.

It was a beautiful autumn day, two days before Halloween, and I was enthralled by the weekend barbecue atmosphere we enjoyed with some real oldies playing in the background. The song "Stand by Me" started playing when I felt compelled to sit down and contact T to tease him about how great my Halloween ghost stories were going to be. To my surprise, I had a negative response all day. This was extremely out of the ordinary, to say the least. I didn't overreact because there had to have been times when he was not on air although, 'til this day, I honestly can't recall a day when he wasn't. Halloween came and went, and *nothing*—no response, just dead air. I was a bit distraught and very concerned about the only true friend I had. I left my radio on all hours of day and night and every penny of my paychecks went to boosting my signal with bigger and better antennae, equipment, and so on. I tried tirelessly to contact T to no avail, and even faked sick days just to try all day to get some contact. I was an empty shell of a person and became even more introverted and self-reliant than before, with taking care of and raising my younger brothers as my only other concern.

It had been about three months and seven days since the last contact. And one night, after putting my brothers to bed, I sat myself in my chair and began broadcasting with every fiber of my soul, my sense of hope hanging by a thread. After an hour or so, I remember lowering my head in despair while a single tear fell from my eye and I transmitted, "T ... I miss you so much, brother."

Then I heard a voice, then static, then the garbled voice again, as if it were such a weak transmission that static was always in the background. I remember thinking, *This is impossible. My equipment is incredible.*

I shot forward and shouted, "T! T! Is that you? Come in! Come in! Please ... please ... I miss you! Please!"

I heard his static-covered voice respond, "Tony ... my ... name is ... Tony."

I screamed, with tears in my eyes, "I miss you, Tony! Where are you?! What happened to you?!"

Through static, he replied, "Join us on the radio ... We ... need ... you ..."

I replied, "I will, tell me how to find you, Tony! I will go!" There was a long pause muffled by the cacophony of static. Then I heard the words, "Not ... yet. This is T ... signing ... off."

I felt a tremor within me that was soul-destroying. It's like you've been asleep after suffering the loss of a loved one or losing your first love, and you're suddenly ripped back into the reality of that loss, waking to the torment and anguish of being. It's like every sad emotion floods back into your mind, and your inner soul struggles to sustain itself.

A few minutes passed as I sat there staring at my desk, listening to the faint static, when another voice came through. "Hello? Say again?" he said. I recognized the voice right away: it was Jim, T's dad. I shot up from my seat and shouted into the mic: "Jim! Jim! Come in! What happened to T? Where is he? Is he okay?!"

He replied, "Hmm? What is wh—who this? Whadya want?"

I said, "Jim, Please! I'm trying to get a hold of T, where is he? Is he okay?"

"What? Is this a joke? Who is this?" Jim asked in confusion.

"Is your name Jim, or not?" I shouted in frustration. "Where is your son T? Is he all right?"

"My son's name is Tony. Only his friends called him T 'cause it got underneath my son's skin. But you must be confused with some other person .... My son died about twenty-five years ago. Sorry, young fella."

"Wha ...? Th—that's not ..." I couldn't even muster the mental capacity to complete my sentence as my head swirled in clouds of sadness, confusion, and false hope. I tried to think of something to say or ask to make it all not true or disprove this heart-wrenching information. I shakily muttered, "How'd he die, sir? If you don't mind."

"Well, all the facts come from his buddy who survived that day. Tony and his buddy would always go down there and play in them woods. And ... well, the story, as his buddy tells it, is that they was playin' army like they loved to do, and in between their pretend battle, they found a tattered old radio flyer wagon flipped upside down. They turned it over, excited 'bout what they could do with it, and they felt like it was Christmas morning, 'cause they found a couple of walkie-talkies underneath the damn thing. They turned them on and both walkies worked fine. Those two kids spent the whole damn day playin' with their new-found treasures.

"When they was takin a break, 'round evenin' some-time, they heard a faint sobbing comin' from a nearby creek; it was barely audible over the creek and general noises from them woods, but they went to go see what it was. They came across a little girl, 'bout their age, in a tattered blue dress with quite a big scrape on her leg that was bleedin' pretty good, and she was cryin' gently. My boy asked her if she was hurt and if she was lost, and she said yes, I can't find my way home. My boy asked, where is it? She says it's a few blocks into town.

"My boy, I guess was wantin' to be the hero of the day, said he'd take her into town, but his buddy said no way, no how. So Tony said fine, ya big baby, go on home. I'll take her myself. Just keep yer walkie-talkie on you and we can still communicate.

"So apparently the little girl flashed a slight grin and seemed pleased to my son obliging. She upped herself in the wagon and both of them boys went off in their separate directions with the walkies turned on.

"For the next forty-five minutes or so, the boys was chattin' back 'n' forth to make sure everythin's all right, and 'bout this time, my son's walkie started cutting out and gettin' staticky and whatnot. And, well, his buddy said that what he heard was my boy sayin' somethin' like, 'Just 'bout there now,' then there was static for 'bout another ten minutes or so. The last thing he heard was m ... my boy scream, then static for a minute, then the last thing he heard over that walkie was what sounded like a giggle from a little girl. Like I said, this whole account of these events is comin' from his buddy's mouth, so that's all I have to go on in m ... my boy ... missin."

Jim's voice started to crack and I could tell this was very painful for him, and for me. My jaw was dropped in a silent scream as I listened to him, all the while, my head was swirling in the cloudiness of disbelief and horror as I was thinking, *This simply cannot be what I am hearing ... this can't be real!*

Jim continued, "Well, of course, we got the police involved, and they did their searchin' and investigatin' and whatnot. Those damn fools was askin' me all sorts of dumb shit questions 'bout my boy and his home life, like I's the suspect or somethin'. But in the end, my boy was never found, and the only thing that was even close to a clue 'bout what happened to him was somethin' we saw during the search.

"Like I said, we went out over to the last place the two boys were together, out in them woods where they was playin', and we searched for anything to help find my missin' boy. After some time goin' 'round in circles, well, I got fed up and asked his buddy what direction he went off in to take that little girl home. He slowly looked around and pointed in a direction, and I took his arm, and we walked and searched for some time.

Truth be told, I was givin' up hope on findin' my boy when all of a sudden, his buddy stopped dead in his tracks and I watched the color drain from his face. He was just starin' at somethin', so I ask him what's wrong. He pointed slow and stiff-like and I could see his lips trembling a bit. I looked over to where he was pointing and saw somethin' that I couldn't quite make out. So we slowly walked over so I could get a better look at what the hell we was lookin' at, and as we came up to it, I realized that it was a wagon ... the same goddamn wagon from the story that he done told us.

"The wagon was beat to shit and flipped upside down. I told his buddy to wait here and I walked up to it and lifted it up and flipped it over. As it flipped, I jumped back and my blood froze. His buddy let out a squeal but cupped his hands over his mouth to silence hisself. We were both starin' at a filthy, torn-up blue dress like he said that little girl was wearin'. Right next to it, halfway buried in the soil, was my boy's walkie-talkie. I picked it up and got nothin', batteries were dead. They was dead as the hope I had left in my heart of ever findin' ... m ... my boy."

I gulped. "I'm sorry for your loss, sir, and I don't really know how to explain this, but I met a very dear friend through this CB radio and over time, he's become my best friend. My .... only friend. I know this sounds crazy, but I swear on everything I love that I believe I've been communicating with your son." My voice started to crack as tears started to stream out uncontrollably, but I continued. "I ... I just can't handle the fact that he might *not* be real ... He cannot be a ghost! I mean, we've talked every day, and he's like a brother to me!"

"Well, dry yer eyes, now, son," Jim responded, "and I'm also sorry for your loss, but I don't rightly believe you've been conversing with *my* son. It's ... it's just one hell of a coincidence, ya know, it's all just big hat, no cattle. And how in the hell ya knew my name when I heard this here CB goin' off, I surely don't know, but maybe your buddy is still around somewhere. He might be on vacation or somethin'. Did he mention anything 'bout leavin' town when y'all last spoke??"

I gulped and weakly replied, "No, the last thing that I ever heard from him was 'Join us on the radio.' After I had screamed that I would join him, he replied, 'Not yet ... T, signin' off ...'"

"That was the last thing I ever heard from him." Jim said nothing for a moment, then he muttered, "Wh ...What the hell? Well, I'll be goddamned, son. My boy was a youngin', but we always taught him the values of a hard workin' man, and I done got him a job cleanin' and doin' janitor type stuff at my good friend's workplace. It was a radio station! I ... I just don't ... Listen, son, my heads a-spinnin', and it's tough to talk 'bout my boy. I'm sorry, but I better let you go for now."

"Wait!" I shouted. "Before you go, sir, I just got a question, if that's all right with you."

"Go ahead, son," he said.

"Well, I'm broadcasting on this CB today, sir, because I was hoping in a desperate attempt to hear from my best friend T ... but, sir, how did I get in contact with *you*?"

There was a brief pause and then Jim sighed. "That's exactly the thang that's fixin' to eat up my brain. Ya see, when my boy went missin', it done tore a hole in me and my wife's hearts, so we decided to leave my son's room and all his belongings exactly the way they was when he disappeared. And ... well ... tonight, I was watchin' TV and relaxin' when I heard a ruckus comin' from my boy's room. I went in his room to get a better listen and heard you screamin' through this here CB radio. But the thing that's confoundin' me is that this CB has been turned off from the time my boy passed and I tell ya now, may God strike me dead ... This damn radio is *still turned off, as we speak*!"

Static interference started to garble Jim's transmission, and something told me my time was extremely limited. Yet, this was too much for my mind to handle, and the icy cold feeling of pins and needles had been constant throughout the whole conversation, to the point where I was freezing cold and my teeth chattering. Trying to maintain my composure, I asked, "Wh ... What ever happened to your son's buddy, sir?"

"Well, like I said, there weren't anybody ... *static* ... believed ... *static* ... his story, so he went ... *static* ... some therapy and such ...."

The static interference was getting worse and it was hard to make out any coherence. I struggled to listen fervently as he continued. "Last thing I heard, son, was

he ... *static* ... ended ... mental facility ... *static* ... claimin'
insanity ... *static* ... done committed suicide ..."

That was it ... end transmission. Nothing but static
remained and I've never heard from Jim again, nor have
I ever successfully contacted anybody on that fre-
quency, and believe me, I tried obsessively.

My life over the decades that followed has mainly
consisted of me trying to make any sense out of this
lifelong tragedy. I have read hundreds of paranormal
books, articles, journals, archives, and basically any
resource that delves into the unknown or spiritual
consciousness in order to not only find out who my
best friend was, but also what happened to him. Or
was he even real? I have had my heart broken over the
loss of my best friend, especially in such a manner as
these experiences gave me absolutely no closure or
understanding. I would compare it to meeting the love
of your life and living blissfully together until one day
they are taken from you, with no explanation or insight,
and you are just expected to carry on with life, without
them, as if everything were normal.

I have been not only been accused of being too
obsessed with the supernatural, paranormal, and even
simple ghost stories, but I have also lost many jobs and
employment over this perspective. I am currently jobless once again but in my mind, I know that God and
my faith and perseverance will eventually guide me to
the truth and back to my dear friend. Rest in peace,
Tony.

# CHAPTER 8
# DARK & DISTURBED

Now that we've established that not all hauntings are done by flesh-rotting zombies and demons hell-bent on stealing the soul of your dog, let's get to some stories where the entity in question may possess some of these qualities. Coming out and sharing encounters of this type takes an incredible amount of courage, as while these do classify as some of the scariest experiences, they are often quickly dismissed by others as too outlandish to be real. The reality of these nightmarish encounters, however, is that they are all too real and those who were involved have to mentally deal with the outcome for a lifetime. Experiences like these can be incredibly terrifying, confusing, and scarring. They also show just how dark the ghost family tree can get.

## MAN ON FIRE

When the dead return in the form of a ghost or another supernatural entity, we often envision a glowing or semi-transparent being displaying their "best" living form. That is the PG version of hauntings that many of us want to believe. We don't want to imagine ourselves returning to the world as ghosts that appear as they did immediately before departing the mortal plane, especially if that departure was under tragic circumstances. Fortunately, it's not that often that a haunting is reported with the ghost resembling a zombie cast member of a horror movie. That is not the case in this chilling account of the supernatural, however.

A child witnesses a horrific accident, only to be scared by what appears to be the flame-ravaged body of the victim following him home to torment him in the night.

While we don't question the writer or his experience, we do question if this apparition was, in fact, the victim returning to haunt a reliable witness to the tragedy. Based on the thousands of stories and experiences we've learned from over the years, this doesn't seem to be the traditional appearance most ghosts take upon returning from a disfiguring death. Often, a "best version" seems to be what appears, if the ghost appears in a physical form at all.

What occurs in this story does, however, seem to be a tactic that many non-human ghosts have taken, with the goal of psychologically disturbing and frightening those in its path. The non-human entity with darker intent will take on whatever form it knows will most disturb its intended target. This is often extremely confusing to those who have the unfortunate experience of witnessing it and can result in an incredibly troubling situation. Jesus shares his story with us:

> I'd like to preface this story by saying that there are two incidents in my life that have greatly shaped the

person that I am. Not to get too personal, but I suffer greatly from anxiety and depression, and I can trace the origins of these issues to two events, both of which happened less than a year apart. The story I'm about to share is one of those.

My family was practically nomadic for the first few years of my life. We had tried to make a go of it in the Los Angeles area and found that life there was much harder than life in Texas, so we decided that we would move back and try to plant some roots. We packed up all our meager belongings and hit the highway, hoping that we would finally be able to have a better life. It was as we were on the road in Arizona that a car wreck halted our advance.

This car had flipped over onto its roof and several people, my dad included, got out to help the driver. The car was in such bad shape that getting the driver out proved to be a near impossible task. This was long before the time of cellphones, so getting emergency services out was a bit of an ordeal. Someone had set out to do so, but it would be a while before someone would come out. My momma and I were instructed to sit in the car while my dad tried to help.

They were trying to keep the driver calm when the unexpected happened: the car caught fire. Everyone went into scramble mode and tried their hardest to free the driver, but their efforts went unrewarded. Flames consumed the vehicle and the air soon filled with the pained screams of the driver as the fire robbed him of his life. The crowd could only watch in horror as the scene unfolded, myself included. I was staring out of the car window in shock at what I was witnessing. My momma told me not to look, but the sight was the least disturbing aspect of it.

There are two things about this event in particular that I would never forget. One was the screams, screams that begged for either death or salvation, screams that begged to be free from the pain and anguish they were in. The second was the smell. Gasoline mixed with burning rubber and another scent, a scent that is indescribable to those who have never smelled it, the scent of burning flesh. By the time the paramedics got there, the flames had consumed both the car and the driver within. The police showed up, too, to take a statement from all the witnesses, something that made my dad nervous because he was an illegal immigrant and didn't feel comfortable around the highway patrol. The jaws of life were employed and they ripped the car apart like a tuna can. All they extracted was a smoldering corpse.

After giving a statement to the highway patrol, we were on our way. We drove in complete silence for several hours until we arrived back into Texas. We moved back to Abilene, where an uncle had opened his home to us and let us stay indefinitely. We tried to put the situation behind us. It took us a few days to settle in but things got back to normal—well, what we considered normal for us. I was enrolled in school for the first time. We planned to stop wandering, and that was a positive step toward that endeavor. Unfortunately, that entailed putting an extra degree of stress upon me. Most of us know what it feels like to be the new kid at school; add to that the fact that I couldn't speak a lick of English and there was a storm of anxiety building up within me.

Being the odd man out took a toll on me, and I found myself becoming introverted due to the embarrassment of not being able to speak English. My room became my safe haven and I found myself spending more and time in there alone. The peace that I felt in there didn't last long. It might've been the additional stress or the feelings of seclusion that I was beginning to develop, but I started to feel uncomfortable in my room. I would sit in there playing with my toys, and suddenly I began to feel an oppressive force descend upon me. There was no obvious source but I could feel it all around me. It felt tangible, like how you can feel humidity stick to your skin on a hot summer day. At times, it would make me feel physically ill. My stomach would lurch and I'd get a persistent feeling of butterflies that would often lead to me vomiting. The more it happened, the more worried my parents became.

Eventually I was taken to the doctor to see if was sick. The conclusion was that there was nothing physically wrong with me and instead it was suggested that I see a counselor, as the doctor suspected I was dealing with anxiety.

I don't know if y'all know a lot about Mexican culture, especially as it sits with the older generations. To see a counselor was to admit that there was something mentally wrong with me, and to admit that would be a great shame. My dad decided that I would just get over it, that it was just a phase. In the end, nothing was done and I was left to suffer.

I would sit in my room with that heavy feeling of oppression suffocating me until I was forced out. I began to avoid being in my room if I could help it. I would watch TV in the living room, or play outside by myself, just to keep myself from having to go in there. Unfortunately, that didn't work come nightfall. I had to sleep in there. I had tried sleeping in the living room but I was reprimanded for it.

I remember the night things changed. I was lying in bed trying to sleep when I started to feel something in the room with me. I looked around and found that I was alone, yet I could feel something at the foot of my bed leering at me, like a predator about to strike. I pulled the blankets over my head, the best defense that any child has. I could still feel it, though; it was still there, right at the foot of my bed. There was no sleep that night. That thing had me trapped under my own blankets with only fear to keep me company.

When the morning came, I was more than happy to get to school and away from my room. Of course, I got in trouble for sleeping in class, but it was the only sleep I managed to get. I got an earful from my parents when I got home and was ordered to the one place I absolutely didn't want to be: my room. As soon as I opened the door, I could feel the heaviness descend upon me. I quickly made for the bed, got under my blankets, and hid. I wasn't sure what I was hiding from. The feeling during the day was much different than what it was at night. It felt scattered, like it was everywhere. It wasn't just fixed to one spot like it had been the night before, but it did feel a little less intense this way and it became borderline bearable. I decided that if I watched TV or played that I might be able to tune it out completely. I had moderate success during the day, but the night was a different story. I laid myself to bed that night and pulled the blankets over my head. I don't know if I hadn't noticed it the night before, but I began to hear the floorboards creak in my room. It started from the corner of the room and stopped right at the foot of my bed. Again, I could feel whatever it was watching me with a fierce intensity. All I could do was hide. I didn't want to face whatever horror was waiting for me outside the blankets. It was a test of endurance; my bladder was my worst enemy in this situation, and whatever was at the foot of my bed did not relent in its torment of me. Eventually I had to give in.

I ripped myself out of bed and ran for the bathroom, trying my damnedest not to look to the foot of my bed. I did my thing and prepared to face a new challenge, getting back into my room while avoiding whatever was in there. I steeled my resolve and charged into my room, throwing myself under my blankets. The thing wasn't there anymore; the feeling of something standing at the foot of my bed was gone, so I took the opportunity to get some much-needed sleep. I woke the next morning to notice that the feeling of oppression had returned, though it was back to that all-encompassing feeling as opposed to the right-at-the-foot-of-the-bed feeling. I could live with that. I dressed and eventually headed to school, where I didn't struggle to stay awake after getting to sleep for once. I went home and avoided my room as much as I could, which was fairly easy, as my parents both worked and I had the house to myself until about six or so. Inevitably, the time came where I would have to go to bed.

That familiar feeling would be waiting on me each and every time I went up to my room for bed. It went on for several weeks like this and eventually, it just became part of life. I got used to it given enough time; even something like this eventually fits in to the routine after a while. I don't know if it was because of that, but things slowly began to change. The presence was always there during the day, but at night it changed. I remember lying in bed that night with a feeling of anxiety tying my stomach in knots. I knew something was different, I could feel it. I waited for the familiar sound of footsteps and I wasn't disappointed. When I looked, however, that's when I noticed that things weren't the same.

I could see the figure of a person standing at the foot of my bed. It looked like it was made of smoke. It was nebulous like a cloud, but blacker than any storm cloud I've ever seen. It churned violently, like it was struggling to hold its form. It stood there and even though it had no noticeable eyes, I knew it was staring at me. I covered myself with my blanket again. Now that it had a physical manifestation, I felt like it could get to me.

Unfortunately, my blanket was my only defense mechanism at the time, as even my voice failed me. I lay in bed trembling, unable to get any kind of sleep. It's funny how one change can add another layer of fear, can magnify things one hundred–fold. I couldn't wait for the morning to come, but that seemed like an eternity away.

When morning finally did come, the figure vanished and the feeling I had grown accustomed to returned. I told my mom and dad about it but I wasn't taken seriously; they saw it as me trying to get out of going to school. Even in light of previous things that had happened, they still had trouble taking me at my word. I resorted to trying to sneak out of my room in the middle of the night and sneaking back in before my parents woke up just so I wouldn't have to see that smoke man again. The first night I attempted it, I saw the smoke man standing in my doorway watching me. After that night, I began to close the door. Eventually I got caught and had to return to my room. Mom would even check up on me in the middle of the night to make sure I was in my room. Apparently, she didn't notice the smoke man. It was always there when she would check on me, but she would never comment about it.

I dealt with that thing for almost a month, but I didn't even get a chance to get used to it before it changed. The cocoon of smoke cracked one night. The smoke man appeared one night, as it had done so many times before. The difference was that this time, the smoke drifted away and what was left was a man, just a run of the mill, average type of man. He was short

and a bit pudgy with dark brown hair. He had this look
of intense anger and hatred, and now that I could see
his eyes, I knew that it was all directed toward me. I
met his gaze and was immediately transfixed. My body
would not move. I was frozen to my spot in bed with
this man staring me down with a look of rage. I had
never in my life experienced that sort of emotion; it was
terrifying. We were engaged in a staring contest that I
did not want to be a part of. It lasted all night, and as
the sun began to peek over the horizon, he turned and
walked back into the corner of the room before vanishing. I cried; my pent-up fear rushed out all at once,
and I cried.

Momma came and checked on me because she
heard me crying. By this time, she had genuinely started
to worry and had begun to believe that something was
indeed going on. She assumed I was having night terrors and tried to convince my dad that I needed help.
He told me that I would get over it and that I didn't
need help and that was that. Momma allowed me to
sleep in the living room even though she didn't think
my room was the problem. I gladly accepted and that
seemed to help the situation. After several weeks of
this, it was decided that I should return to my room. I
wasn't pleased with this decision, but my dad insisted
that I was being ridiculous and that I needed to grow
up. I sat in my bed that night, the feeling of oppression
that I had come to know so intimately hanging in the
air like a fog. Anxiety gripped me, twisting my stomach
in knots. My eyes were fixated upon the corner of the

room where I knew that angry man would be making his appearance. The minutes ticked by and I felt like I was going to have a panic attack.

He came. He appeared to walk out of the corner of the room, his face contorted in a look of rage that seemed to have intensified with my absence. His eyes locked with mine and he began that familiar walk to the foot of my bed. I was frozen in fear and despite everything inside me screaming at me to run, to hide, I couldn't. We engaged in the same staring match we had all those nights ago. This time, however, things were different.

Smoke began to billow up from around him. He opened his mouth, and from within, there erupted the most anguished scream I had ever heard. It echoed through the room, the pain held within it incomprehensible to my young mind. I hoped my momma or my dad would hear it, that they would rush in and save me, but they didn't. It seemed like this show was only for me. As he screamed, the flesh on his face began to split and a familiar scent filled the air, the smell of burning rubber and human flesh I had smelled back on that highway. Cracks appeared in his skin and what I assume was blood began to ooze out. His skin began to blister and blacken, the blood on his face starting to boil as if someone were taking a blue torch to him. His eyes seemed to melt away, shriveling up in their sockets to leave hollowed-out pits. Flesh began to slough off and hit the ground in charred chunks. What was left was a skull with bits of blackened flesh clinging tenaciously to it. All the while, he continued to scream as he was reduced to a burnt-out husk. He cried for what seemed like hours and when his screams stopped, mine started.

Momma rushed in upon hearing me and tried to console me as I cried and screamed. I couldn't be consoled and my screaming didn't stop until I passed out. When I woke, I was questioned thoroughly. I told my mom everything that had happened and she was insistent that I had a just had a nightmare. That is until my dad, who had been listening intently, pointed out the two burnt spots on the wooden floor at the foot of my bed. Momma sought religious council and she finally received it. A priest blessed both me and the home. Just for added insurance, I was also taken to a *bruja* for a blessing from an alternative source. Blessings were nice and all, but I had watched a man burn to death and no amount of blessings could undo that.

The man stopped coming. I never saw him again. My dad asked me what the man had looked like and when I described him, he became suddenly somber. I later learned that I described, to the last detail, the man that had died on the highway on our way back to Texas. I don't know why he showed his last moments to me, why he was so angry at me, or what caused him to attach himself to me. I'm not even sure it was him; maybe it was something already in that house that was preying on a little boy who witnessed something he didn't understand. Something that wanted to weaken and oppress me, to keep me in a state of perpetual fear. Whatever the case, it left a scar; it filled me with an anxiety that persists to this day, so if that was its goal, then it was successful.

Even though the haunting was over with, I was still haunted. I know I said that I never saw that man again but that was lie. Even now, as a thirty-four-year-old man, when I close my eyes I can still see that man burning away to nothing. I can still hear his screams of pain, and worst of all, I can still smell the scent of burning flesh.

# BILLY

If there were ever a contributor to our show who led a haunted life, Oscar would be the poster child. Over the years, Oscar has shared several stories with us, some of the most haunting stories that we have ever heard. His stories include one about a zombie ghost clown who has tormented his family since an accident outside of their apartment building when he was a child. The story was featured on our broadcast several times and picked up by several other podcasts due to its haunting and extreme nature.

Oscar has what we would call a gift. Not all gifts are wonderful, however; he has more of the "fruitcake at Christmas" gift. To some, this "gift" might be a nice thought, but to the person on the receiving end, it might not be such an enjoyable experience. Oscar is an individual who seems to have a sensitivity level far beyond most and is able to pick up on not only the good, but often the dark side of the undead. He has had experiences with entities that were once human and roam the earth, along with several others that never were human yet still exist with the sole purpose of tormenting the living.

In this submission from Oscar, one that we have never shared on the air, he takes us for a jog down an infamous path, a running path with a storied history of hauntings and tragic consequences. Some can argue that these consequences may have been caused by the ghosts that haunt the area. This is just one of Oscar's many haunted stories.

Like most people, I hate running, especially at night. I try to run at least four miles a day, and I always take the same path around Lake Cliff Park and the Houston Street Bridge. Lake Cliff is ancient, with a huge lake in the middle, and the park itself is about two miles long. The park is surrounded by old Victorians and a wooded area with sloping willows that bend toward the lake. The Houston Street Bridge, which spans at least two miles, is a majestic structure built in the early 1900s. The bridge's 1920s architectural design has not changed in decades. Together, the bridge and park make up six miles of beautiful Texas scenery, which makes my run a little better.

I get out of work sort of late, so I end up running in the dark. I don't mind; nothing can scare me. One night I was running like I always do. I had just started to run across the Houston bridge. I looked up to enjoy the Dallas Skyline, when suddenly I felt someone behind me. That's ordinary; everyone is faster than me when I'm running at night. So I moved to the side to let the other runner pass me. I could feel the person behind me, and I didn't have to turn around because I could hear him. I felt like the runner was next to me, so I turned to say "hi." To my surprise, there was no one there. I didn't pay much attention to it. Whatever it was, I didn't want it to follow me home. I have experience in things like this.

I told whatever it was it wasn't welcome, and I didn't want it around me. So, I kept running, this time a little faster, occasionally looking back to make sure whatever it was wasn't following me. It wasn't the first time I felt something wicked on the bridge. The Houston Bridge was notorious as a spot for dumping bodies in the Trinity River basin. The bridge was also known as a spot for strange sightings of children and half-naked women, which have been known to cause fatal accidents. I see what you're thinking, every bridge has some local urban legend, but I can tell you, this bridge is very haunted.

My grandfather took the bus from Oak Cliff to downtown every night, and he would say the devil was on the bridge, so he considered the bridge cursed. I felt not one but multiple entities all along my running route, but nothing was more evil than what I named Billy. Billy felt like a curious child. I never saw him directly, but Billy was no child; I don't even think he was ever human.

I first experienced Billy along the darkest route in the park next to the bridge. I knew he was around when the stink of decay hit me like a ton of brick. At first, I thought it was a dead animal somewhere, but this odor was different. It seemed to follow me up to the bridge. Then the flies started to appear. Not your normal flies; I'm talking about the big horse flies, the type you see around dead bodies. The flies would fly close to my mouth, almost like they were trying to go into my lips. *Buzz, buzz,* they hovered by my ears and all around my face. *Run faster,* I told myself, as I did the sign of the holy cross on my forehead. *Not today, Billy*, as the smell disappeared behind me. He wasn't the only ghost I experienced while running, but he was the strongest. That's why I knew it wasn't a human spirit, but something more primal and ancient. How do I know this? Well, let me tell you, it's not the first time I felt something demonic, and it won't be the last. It's not something you tend to forget.

Unfortunately, there are other ways it can follow you home. The day started like any other typical day at work. Everything seemed perfect for a weekday. The afternoon was an extra beautiful sunny day. Suddenly, I received a call from my daughter. It started with an innocent question.

"The train isn't running today. I think I am going to walk home from school, is that cool, Dad?" To walk from her high school in downtown Dallas to our house would be about a four-mile walk through downtown, across the Houston Bridge, and into Lake Cliff Park. It was a beautiful day in Dallas, after all, so I told her, "Sure, go ahead." It wasn't a big deal, I thought. It was the first time she'd ever walked home. I got busy at work and soon forgot about her call. She finally texted

me that she got home safe. She said she had taken
the bridge and decided to stroll by the lake. "Good," I
thought. I was glad she made it home safe, so I started
to plan my nightly run. Finally, work was over, and I
went back home like I always do.

I walked into my house and headed straight into the
kitchen to make a sandwich. I noticed flies all over my
house. "Olivia!" I shouted, "Why did you leave the door
open, now we have a lot of flies in the kitchen." The
flies were big black horse flies. Something was strange,
I could feel it in my bones; I couldn't put my finger on
what it was. I noticed a pungent smell coming from
the kitchen, the kind of smell that sticks to your skin. I
recognized the stench of death. I knew something was
horribly wrong with my house. I followed the odor to
the trash. *Maybe the kids left food overnight?* But the
trash was empty. I followed the smell to the hallway.
The scent of death just lingered in the lobby.

My daughter walked out of her room, curious about
what I was doing. "Is it a dead rat?" she asked. I turned
to give her a reply when I noticed something out of
place. The light from my daughter's room cast her
reflection against the wall. That's when I noticed the
second shadow behind her. *Two shadows? Maybe she
has a guest?* I tried to rationalize. It had the shape of a
teenage boy the same height as my daughter. As soon as
I noticed the shadow, it disappeared into the room.

My daughter saw me looking at something else.
"What's wrong, Dad?" I quickly replied, "There's something behind you." She looked around slowly; then she

quickly turned back. There was nothing. "Stop creeping me out, Dad," she yelled at me.

I smiled, and I said I was kidding and walked away, but I wasn't. I don't usually tell anyone, especially my children, that ghosts are around, but something was different about this one. Something wicked had followed my daughter home that day.

The day passed and the flies started to build up on the windows. The more I sprayed the flies with bug spray, the more flies showed up. I knew there was something in my house. The night passed, and morning came. Soon my wife and kids went to school and work. I worked from home that day. I decided that I needed to confront whatever had invaded my house before it decided to stay. My bedroom is upstairs, and my daughter's room is located downstairs on the other side of the house.

I knew the only way to contact the entity was to take a nap. The dead talk to me when I am asleep. So I lay down just to rest my eyes. I pulled the bed covers over my head, with my laptop next to me just in case someone from work decided to instant message me with a question. Soon after I fell asleep, I woke up by a door slam coming from my daughter's room.

"Olivia, is that you?" I yelled from underneath my covers. "NOOOOOO," came the reply in a slow moan. I felt a shiver down my backbone; I knew I contacted the demon. The cry seemed to continue getting louder and louder. Then I heard the dull clang of feet slowly walking up the stairs. *Clang, clang, clang,* it walked closer and closer.

"NOOOOOO," it kept repeating louder and louder as it got closer to my room. My door slowly opened, with the longest creaking sound. Now the footsteps were in my room. Suddenly, the intruder ran across my room and jumped on top of me. I was still under the sheets, frozen in place by fear. Its weight crushed me. It felt like a grown man jumped on me. Its breath moved the bed covers, and the odor of death made my eyes water. "NOOOOOOO," it screamed in my face. Then the entity slowly whispered, "Billy." My skin began to burn with anxiety. This crazy laugh came out of all four walls and a fear I haven't felt in a long time took hold of me.

"Get off me, you're not welcome in my house!" I yelled from the top of my lungs. I felt its hands and body on top of me, scratching and clawing at the sheets, like an animal trying to dig a hole in the ground. I started to pray, and I asked Jesus to save me. As soon as I mentioned Jesus, it stopped and disappeared. I quickly got up and checked every inch of my room. I went downstairs to check on my daughter's room, and nothing. The entity had vanished from my house. I didn't tell my family because I feared they might accidently invite Billy back.

So I decided to change my running route. I learned my lesson: never let something follow me or my family home again. I am sure Billy is still out there, underneath the Houston Bridge, waiting for someone to follow home. If you want to experience Billy for yourself, then you should run my route when the sun goes down. I am sure Billy will be waiting for you under the Houston Bridge. He's always there, waiting to make a new friend.

# CONCLUSION

We've come to the conclusion of this book, yet we feel like we have only touched the very surface when it comes to examining the thousands of ghost types that have been reported on our program. We often look at the paranormal as a very dysfunctional family tree. Every time you think you've come to the top of the tree, suddenly another story comes in that makes you realize there are several other secret siblings that create another branch you didn't know existed. These discoveries lead us down paths of even more unexplained and intriguing possibilities in the supernatural world.

Will these branches ever lead to an end, or a clear definition as to what a ghost is? We doubt it.

We feel that the world of the paranormal is far more complex and vast than any of us can comprehend. It seems to be a world of the once living and never living, with every entity on the other side having its own unique abilities and skills. The more one tries to group an entity into a certain category, the more futile and inaccurate that practice seems to become.

So, what is the ultimate goal of our book or the podcast we share? Is it to prove that ghosts exist? No. We're already operating on the idea that they are certainly out there, so we have nothing to prove on that question. Is it to debunk a story or account of the paranormal? No. Everyone who encounters these beings knows what happened to them was paranormal; claiming to have a better understanding of an experience we were not present for would be ignorant and foolish.

Our goal in this book and on our podcast is to provide an outlet for the paranormally affected, to show them that they are normal and are not alone. We represent the fact that completely balanced, regular people have unexplained experiences every day, all over the world. It is to show how others have handled such situations and possibly provide some direction and information on what can be done to process the reality that the dead, at times, are still among the living.

A term thrown around when we first started the show was "group therapy for the paranormally affected," and in a way, that's what our show still is. We are not doctors, nor do we give medical advice. Rather, through the telling of shared paranormal experiences, many have found a community of like-minded people who have a common bond: ghosts. Some are good, some are evil, and some are just plain bizarre. The bottom line is that no matter what type of paranormal experience you've had, chances are many, many more have had it, too, and you will hear about it on our show.

So, what has been your experience with the paranormal? Did this book make you recall some experience you'd put on the back shelf of your mind due to fear or anxiety of what others may think? If you have had an experience, we would love to hear about it. Chances are, thousands of others all over the world would also like to hear about your unexplained experience. You may find that taking the time to recount your story is not only freeing to you personally, but it may also help others understand and find peace and closure for their own event. This is why we do what we do.

That is why this book doesn't end here.

The stories continue every day on our podcast, *Real Ghost Stories Online*, which can be found on iTunes, YouTube, and most podcast services. We hope you'll continue to join us on this journey, and we can't wait to hear your story in the next chapter of *Real Ghost Stories Online*.

# ABOUT THE AUTHORS

**Tony & Jenny Brueski** are heard every day around the world in thousands of homes, cars, and offices on their incredibly popular podcast *Real Ghost Stories Online*. Their show is an exciting and often chilling mix of real ghost stories as recounted by the people who experienced them. It's not medical advice, but their show is often referred to as "group therapy for the paranormally affected," as thousands find comfort in the community of like-minded individuals that have discovered their show. *Real Ghost Stories Online* can be downloaded through iTunes, YouTube, and almost any podcast download program. Tony & Jewnny live in the Ozark Mountains with their two girls and no ghosts, just the stories sent in to them every day.